Mobile Learning

Mobile Learning

Special Issue Editor

Maria Uther

MDPI • Basel • Beijing • Wuhan • Barcelona • Belgrade

Special Issue Editor
Maria Uther
University of Wolverhampton
UK

Editorial Office
MDPI
St. Alban-Anlage 66
4052 Basel, Switzerland

This is a reprint of articles from the Special Issue published online in the open access journal *Education Sciences* (ISSN 2227-7102) from 2018 to 2019 (available at: https://www.mdpi.com/journal/education/special_issues/Mobile_Learning)

For citation purposes, cite each article independently as indicated on the article page online and as indicated below:

LastName, A.A.; LastName, B.B.; LastName, C.C. Article Title. *Journal Name* **Year**, *Article Number*, Page Range.

ISBN 978-3-03897-660-8 (Pbk)
ISBN 978-3-03897-661-5 (PDF)

Contents

About the Special Issue Editor

Maria Uther is a Professor of Psychology at the University of Wolverhampton and is the Head of the Centre for Psychological Research. She is a Health Professional Council registered Occupational Psychologist and a British Psychological Society Chartered Psychologist. She has authored numerous peer-refereed journal articles, given keynote talks, and her work has been funded by a variety of sources, including the EPSRC, ESRC, Nuffield Foundation, Nokia Foundation, and Sharp Research Laboratories of Europe. She is a sought-after external consultant on the design and usage of mobile technologies for learning. She has served on numerous scientific committees, including Interspeech, IEEE International Conference on Acoustics, Speech and Signal Processing, and IADIS mobile learning, among others.

Preface to "Mobile Learning"

It is my great pleasure to introduce this edited volume of works on mobile learning. Although my own academic career started within auditory cognitive neuroscience, a series of serendipitous events took me into the field of mobile device usage for learning. Over the years, I have found that although 'nothing much has changed, everything has also changed very much'. Technology has most certainly changed, but the overarching themes remain the same: 'Why would we use mobile devices for learning?' 'Do mobile devices help or hinder learning?' And 'How do we evaluate mobile learning?' The evolution of new technologies has certainly influenced the way that we can answer these questions, and these papers provide useful commentary on the current state of play.

Maria Uther
Special Issue Editor

Editorial

Mobile Learning—Trends and Practices

Maria Uther

Department of Psychology, University of Wolverhampton, City Campus, Wolverhampton, WV1 1LY, UK;
m.uther@wlv.ac.uk

Received: 31 January 2019; Accepted: 2 February 2019; Published: 5 February 2019

Abstract: Mobile learning has become one of the more influential aspects in the field of educational technology given the ubiquity of modern mobile devices and proliferation of educational applications or 'apps' for mobile devices. Within this special issue, there are a range of studies and reviews which cover a breadth of current topics in the field, namely user motivations for using mobile learning, issues in evaluation and domain-specific considerations (e.g., use within language learning or audio-based applications). Together these studies represent the synthesis of a range of methods, approaches and applications that highlight benefits and areas of future growth of mobile technologies.

Keywords: mobile learning; mobile devices; educational technologies

1. Introduction to the Field of Mobile Learning

It is with pleasure that I introduce readers to this special issue of Education Sciences that is dedicated to 'mobile learning'. The field of 'mobile learning' is not intended to denote a special kind of learning. It is simply part of learning. However, the proliferation of mobile devices in our society has allowed mobile devices to be employed to deliver content and activities in which learning can be situated in a broader range of contexts than it has traditionally (e.g., in outdoor settings, in augmented reality, as well as 'just in time' or 'bite-sized' learning such as whilst travelling on public transport, etc.). This special issue encompasses a range of current issues related to motivation for using mobile learning, good practice in implementation and evaluation approaches, as outlined below.

2. The 'why' Question in Mobile Learning

One of the key questions for the use of mobile devices in learning is the 'why' question. Why bother with using mobile learning and what advantages do mobile devices provide in learning? Some key advantages highlighted within the field are the benefits of mobility, 'just-in-time' learning and location-based services, to name a few (see [1–8] for a review). This 'why' question has been probed within Yurdagül and Öz's paper [9], which argues that mobile learning is concerned with the mobility of learners and learning mobility rather than mobility of devices per se. They also highlight the advantages of 'just-in-time' learning in particular, demonstrating rapid access as a key advantage of mobile learning (44%) as well as ease of access (26%) in their survey findings.

Similarly, Elphick's iPilot initiative [10] also explored learner motivations in using mobile devices. The iPilot initiative provided iPads to students on a range of undergraduate programs over a two year pilot period. Surveys of students suggested that the overwhelming majority thought the use of iPads in education improved their digital literacy. Students were also found to be positive about the use of their iPads in learning (e.g., helping creativity in learning, increasing confidence, study efficiency, enjoyment, feeling connected with fellow students, helping communication with others, being more productive, experimenting with new apps and invaluable to studies). Students also do not rate potential disadvantages highly (e.g., low ratings for statements that suggested the iPad would distract or fragment learning). Furthermore, in comparison to non-iPilot students, the students suggested that they were more likely to access learning on the move. Qualitative interviews also suggested that there were advantages in using the iPad that were not directly related to the designed learning applications (e.g., the ability to communicate with other students in group work via messages). In other words, there is evidence that the technical features embedded within mobile devices are useful for learners (even if not expressly designed with pedagogic activities in mind).

3. Do Mobile Devices Help or Hinder Learning?

The other key area is the issue of efficacy of using mobile devices for learning. We want to know whether mobile devices are generally helpful or a hindrance to learning? Two studies address these questions in this issue. The first is Cho et al.'s study [11], which conducted a meta-analysis of the use of mobile language learning technologies to examine two research questions: (1) What is the net effect of using mobile language learning technologies and (2) whether these effects differ as a function of moderator variables such as school level, source of study, context of study, type of test and target language learner type. In a rather robust and detailed quantitative analysis, they found an overall moderate positive effect of mobile device usage on language acquisition and language-learning achievement. Yet at the same time there were moderating influences on student learning outcomes in terms of type of assessment used.

The second study was that of Uther and Ylinen [12] which looked at applications that heavily relied on audio (i.e., music training and speech training). To this end, they compared the user perception of sound quality across devices when physical features are controlled, in order to investigate whether subjective changes affected user preferences for different devices. They found that there were significant differences in subjective sound quality that appeared to be influenced by device type, although the exact pattern of differences was different to previously published work with different demographic samples. Nonetheless, as per other studies, the degree to which these differences actually influenced the learning experience appeared to be limited. Instead, other features such as portability/convenience, etc. appeared to override users' impressions of quality in terms of learner preferences. Hence for learners, the degree to which they are influenced by subjective device/quality differences appears to matter little to their learning experience.

4. How to Evaluate Mobile Learning

Finally, in terms of evaluation: The 'how to evaluate' question, Koole et al. [7] compared two models of mobile learning: FRAME (Framework for Rationale Analysis of Mobile Learning) and the three level evaluation framework (3-LEF). The authors conducted a systematic review of publications referencing the seminal papers that originally introduced the models. In total, 208 publications referencing the FRAME model and 97 publications referencing the 3-LEF were included in their analysis. The authors concluded that these two models/frameworks were likely chosen for reasons other than philosophical commensurability, despite the fact that the FRAME model contains a more social-constructivist (and in latter iterations, sociomaterialist) emphasis and the 3-LEF a more socio-cultural emphasis. The authors posited that researchers may be using these models for reasons such as ease of use, rather than any particular need to evaluate from a particular philosophical position. The paper helpfully outlined potential advantages and disadvantages of each evaluation approach, which researchers may find useful to guide their choice of evaluation framework.

5. Conclusions

The field of mobile learning continues to evolve and yet the key questions of 'Why mobile?', 'Do mobile devices help or hinder learning?' and 'How can mobile learning be evaluated?' are continuing themes in the field. The studies presented in this issue provide a taster of current and continuing research themes in the field and are a useful source of information for practitioners and researchers in the field looking to develop further mobile learning applications.

funding: This research was funded by the Nokia Foundation Visiting Professor Grant, awarded to Professor Uther for a visit to Cicero Learning, University of Helsinki, Finland in 2018.

Acknowledgments: The author acknowledges the assistance of Mari Tervaniemi in practical matters related to accommodating and hosting Uther's research visit to Finland.

Conflicts of Interest: The author declares no conflict of interest.

References

1. Wu, W.H.; Wu, Y.C.J.; Chen, C.Y.; Kao, H.Y.; Lin, C.H.; Huang, S.H. Review of trends from mobile learning studies: A meta-analysis. *Comput. Educ.* **2012**, *59*, 817–827. [CrossRef]
2. Kukulska-Hulme, A. Mobile usability in educational contexts: What have we learnt? *Int. Rev. Res. Open Distance Learn.* **2007**, *8*, 1–16. [CrossRef]
3. Orr, G. A review of literature in mobile learning: Affordances and constraints. In Proceedings of the 6th IEEE International Conference on Wireless, Mobile and Ubiquitous Technologies in Education, Kaohsiung, Taiwan, 12–16 April 2010; pp. 107–111.
4. Jacob, S.M.; Issac, B. The Mobile Devices and its Mobile Learning Usage Analysis. In Proceedings of the International Multiconference of Engineers and Computer Scientists, Hong Kong, China, 19–21 March 2008.
5. Sung, Y.T.; Chang, K.E.; Liu, T.C. The effects of integrating mobile devices with teaching and learning on students' learning performance: A meta-analysis and research synthesis. *Comput. Educ.* **2016**, *94*, 252–275. [CrossRef]
6. Sharples, M.; Pea, R. Mobile learning. In *The Cambridge Handbook of the Learning Sciences*, 2nd ed.; Sawyer, R.K., Ed.; Cambridge University Press: New York, NY, USA, 2015; pp. 501–521.
7. Koole, M.; Buck, R.; Anderson, K.; Laj, D. A Comparison of the Uptake of Two Research Models in Mobile Learning: The FRAME Model and the 3-Level Evaluation Framework. *Educ. Sci.* **2018**, *8*, 114. [CrossRef]
8. Uther, M. Mobile Internet usability: What can 'mobile learning' learn from the past? In Proceedings of the IEEE International Workshop on Wireless and Mobile Technologies in Education, Washington, DC, USA, 29–30 August 2002.
9. Yurdagül, C.; Öz, S. Attitude towards Mobile Learning in English Language Education. *Educ. Sci.* **2018**, *8*, 142. [CrossRef]
10. Elphick, M. The impact of embedded iPad use on student perceptions of their digital capabilities. *Educ. Sci.* **2018**, *8*, 102. [CrossRef]
11. Cho, K.; Lee, S.; Joo, M.-H.; Becker, J. The effects of using mobile devices on student achievement in language learning: a meta-analysis. *Educ. Sci.* **2018**, *8*, 105. [CrossRef]
12. Uther, M.; Ylinen, S. The role of subjective quality judgements in user preferences for mobile learning apps. *Educ. Sci.* **2018**, *9*, 3. [CrossRef]

Article

The Impact of Embedded iPad Use on Student Perceptions of Their Digital Capabilities

Matt Elphick

Academic Quality and Development, University of Winchester, Winchester, Hampshire SO22 4NR, UK; matt.elphick@winchester.ac.uk

Received: 6 June 2018; Accepted: 16 July 2018; Published: 20 July 2018

Abstract: Digital capabilities are recognized as key skills that students must possess to learn and work in our increasingly digital world and have been the subject of a growing focus over recent years. Similarly, smartphones and, to a lesser degree, tablets are now ubiquitous within the student body, and many academics are beginning to leverage these devices for the purposes of learning and teaching in higher education. To further explore the possibilities of mobile technology, the iPilot project was created to explore the effects that embedded iPad use had on undergraduate students' creativity, ability to collaborate with their peers and their perception of their digital capabilities. Focusing on the digital capabilities aspect of the project, this paper explores the results gathered. While the results are mixed, when combined with data taken from the Joint Information Systems Committee (JISC) Digital Experience Tracker, it does appear that using iPads in the university classroom can have a positive impact on certain digital behaviors and students' perceptions of their digital skills.

Keywords: iPads; mobile devices; digital capabilities; digital literacy; higher education

---

1. Introduction

We live in an increasingly digital world, one in which more and more of our daily lives, both personal and professional, are becoming reliant on digital systems. As such, today's students must be equipped with the skills necessary to thrive at university and, beyond that, "to respond with agility over their lifetimes to shifting labor market requirements and fast-changing developments in technology" [1]. As such, digital literacy or, as it is now often referred to, digital capability [2] (please note that the terms are used interchangeably within this paper), is quickly becoming one of the most important skillsets that students require for studying and when entering into the job market.

Marc Prensky's often quoted 'Digital Native, Digital Immigrants, Part 1' proposes that most of our current students think differently to previous generations thanks to growing up surrounded by digital technology. They are, as he puts it, "'native' speakers of the digital language" [3] (p. 5) and as such, appear to have an affinity with digital technology. While some have argued that this view is an "academic form of a 'moral panic'" [4] (p. 783) and others have gone on to fully debunk the idea [5,6], the fact that our students make use of a large range of hardware (laptops, smartphones, tablets) and software (social media, web browsers, games, word processing, and design packages) cannot be denied. However, using digital technology on a frequent basis in their personal lives does not guarantee that our students are gaining the skills necessary for them to thrive in a digital work environment.

JISC defines digital capability as "the capabilities which fit someone for living, learning, and working in a digital society" [7] and provides a framework of the six core elements they believe that a digitally capable individual needs [8]. Based on JISC's latest model, the six elements of digital capability are:

- ICT proficiency (functional skills)
- Information, data and media literacies (critical use)

- Digital creation, problem solving and innovation (creative production)
- Digital communication, collaboration, and participation (participation)
- Digital learning and development (development)
- Digital identity and wellbeing (self-actualizing)

For a number of years JISC has worked on projects creating resources to help institutions [9], academics, and the students themselves [10], embed and improve digital capabilities in the curriculum, and foster digital skills in all involved. Links between teaching excellence and digital capability have been drawn [11], and concerns regarding students' use of technology and conventional study practices have been addressed [12].

Coinciding with, and likely the cause of, this increased focus on digital capabilities is the continued rise of mobile technology, with smartphones especially being ubiquitous among the student body, with 93% of 16–24-year-olds in the UK using one [13] (p. 23). While smartphones may be popular with the student body, it is tablets and their potential for learning and teaching that appear to have caught the attention of the Higher Education (HE) sector, with the Apple iPad being the device most frequently discussed.

Released in April 2010, and having sold over 350 million units worldwide, the iPad is the world's most popular tablet [14]. Many studies have been undertaken to explore the potential that iPads, and tablets more widely, have for learning and teaching. The use of iPads has been seen to increase student engagement [15–19], promote collaboration [16,17], and offer an enhanced learning experience [18] by providing new and creative environments in which students can learn as well as an intuitive touch interface. Despite these benefits, a systematic literature review by Nguyen et al. found that, while use of iPads did enhance the learning experience it did not necessarily lead to better learning outcomes [20].

For the implementation and use of such devices to be successful, time and effort are required by both staff and students [18], and the support provided must be robust and readily available [18,21,22]. Existing pressures on staff time must be considered [19,23] as the creation of learning activities that make use of the devices can be time-consuming. Staff confidence in using, and knowledge of, technology must also be considered [21] as well as their opinions surrounding effective teaching, more widely [24].

2. Materials and Methods

The iPilot project grew out of previous technology-related initiatives at the university, such as FASTECH, which paired staff and students to use technology to overcome problems with assessment [25], and the Mobile Device Scheme, which recruited students with high digital capability skills to mentor staff on the use of mobile devices [26].

The iPilot, which was co-developed between the Learning and Teaching team and the University's Student Union [27], sought to build on these initiatives by exploring the impact that embedded mobile device use had on the student learning experience.

All undergraduate programs were eligible to apply to be a part of the iPilot, with interested parties required to submit a written application and then present their proposals for how the devices would be used to a panel consisting of members of the Learning and Teaching team, the Student Union, and the First Deputy Vice-Chancellor. Based on these presentations seven undergraduate programs were selected to be a part of the project in 15/16, with the same seven continuing with it into 16/17.

Staff and first-year students on these programs were given an iPad mini 2 and case, with the staff being tasked with embedding the use of the devices into the delivery of their modules. The student devices were not provided on loan and were theirs to keep. Prior to the beginning of the semester, all participating staff were invited to attend training sessions facilitated by an Apple Professional Development Authorized Trainer.

480 students received an iPad in 15/16 with a further 469 receiving a device in 16/17 (see Table 1). In total, approximately 100 members of staff were involved in the project. The total number of students participating in the iPilot at the end of the project were as follows:

Table 1. Student numbers.

Program	No. of Students
American Studies	46
Digital Media	46
Law	168
Media and Communication	93
Primary Education	400
Social Work	90
Sport	106
	949

Although the project investigated several different areas relating to iPad use in the classroom, this article will focus on whether the regular and embedded use of the devices had any impact, perceived or otherwise, on students' digital capabilities.

A number of different methods were used to gather information regarding how the students were using the iPads, both inside and outside of the classroom.

Surveys, featuring free-text, five-point Likert scale, and multiple-choice questions, were issued to students at the end of each semester. These surveys were new and designed specifically for the iPilot project. All survey responses were anonymous, and students gave informed consent before participating. Survey questions were designed to reflect the six elements of digital capability, as outlined in JISC's digital capability framework.

Small, semi-structured group interviews were also conducted with students. There was no financial incentive to participate in these group interviews, although pizza was provided.

Lectures and seminars were observed for the author to gain first-hand experience of how the devices were being used in the classroom. Where possible, a class from each program was observed at least once every academic year.

For the purposes of this study, only the survey data will be discussed, however, information gathered from the student interviews and from lecture observations will be used to inform the narrative surrounding the results. During semester 2 of 16/17, JISC launched their Student digital experience tracker [28], and the relevant results from this will also be discussed.

3. Results

The number of responses received by each survey varied depending in which semester it was conducted, with the semester 2 surveys receiving far fewer responses (see Table 2). While it is unclear what caused this variance, the author speculates this may be due to the presence of exams in semester 2 (no centrally organized exams take place in semester 1) causing the students to be under additional time restraints and pressure. The number of responses to each survey can be seen in Table 2, below.

Table 2. Survey responses.

	No. of Responses	Percentage of iPilot Students
Semester 1 15/16	394	82.5%
Semester 2 15/16	166	34.6%
Semester 1 16/17	375	80.0%
Semester 2 16/17	257	54.8%

3.1. Digital Literacy

In the semester 1 survey of each year, students were given a definition of digital literacy ("the capabilities for living, learning and working in a digital society" [29]) and asked to rate how digitally literate they were on a five-point Likert scale. The weighted averages for each year were 4.12 and 4.16 respectively, indicating that the students perceive themselves to be digitally capable individuals.

The fact that students perceive themselves to have such high levels of digital literacy is perhaps unsurprising, given how embedded technology appears to be in their lives. When asked about the devices they already own, the results show that mobile device ownership, particularly that of smartphones and laptops, is prevalent (see Figure 1).

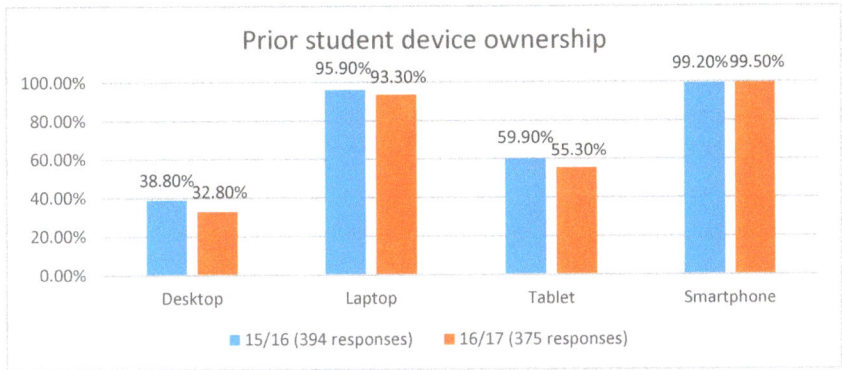

Figure 1. Prior student device ownership.

The data demonstrate that students are prioritizing the ownership of laptops and smartphones over that of desktop computers and tablets. The low ownership of desktop computers could be seen as a move by students to ensure that their technology is portable, although this does not explain why tablet ownership is also comparably small. It is possible that, as tablets bridge the gap in functionality and screen size between laptops and smartphones, many students do not feel a need to possess such a device if they already own the other two. Figure 2, below, provides a more detailed breakdown of tablet ownership by type and confirms that, in this study at least, iPads remain the most popular tablet.

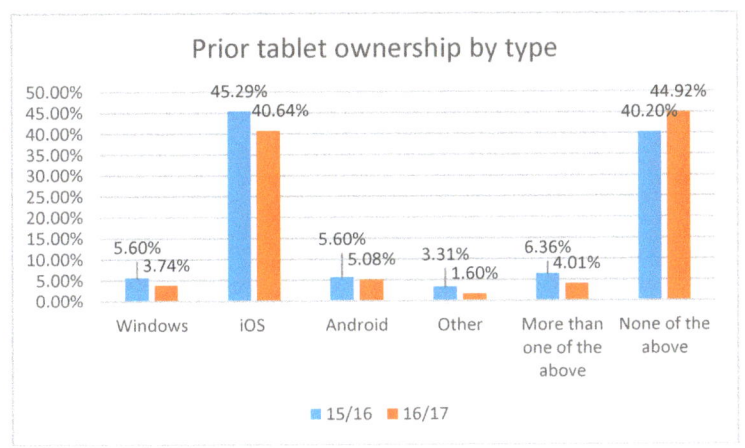

Figure 2. Prior tablet ownership by type.

In semester 2, the students were provided with the same definition of digital literacy and then asked to answer the question, "Do you feel that your digital literacy has developed by having the iPads incorporated into your learning?"

These positive responses (see Figure 3) were echoed in the qualitative comments, with many students claiming that by using the devices for their studies (both inside and outside of the classroom) they had been exposed to new applications and had been presented with new ways of using technology, all of which had a positive impact on their learning.

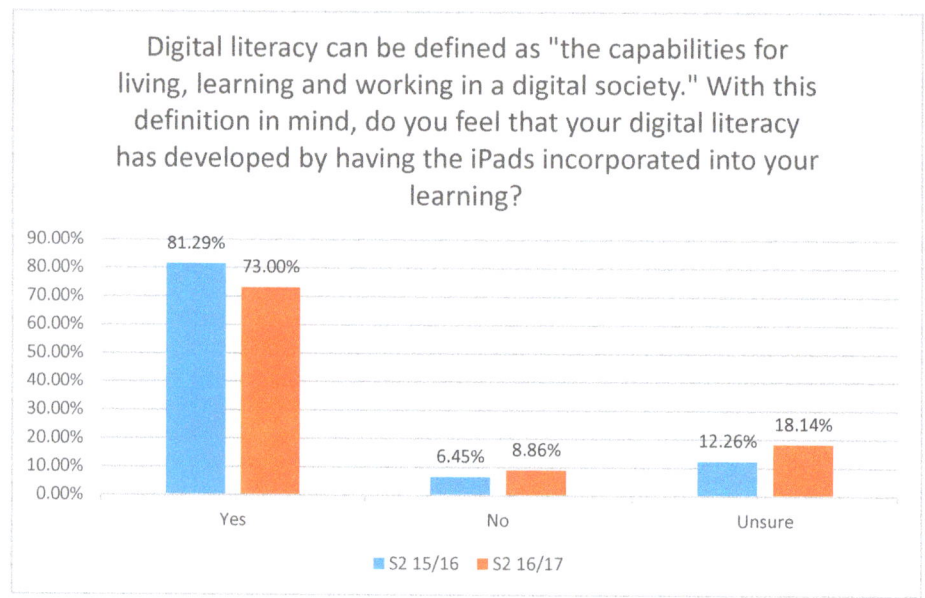

Figure 3. Digital literacy development.

That said, it is clear that some students do not believe, or are unsure whether the devices have had a positive impact on their digital literacy. The qualitative comments relating to these responses report prior, and strong, confidence and competence using technology and, therefore, the students perceived that, although useful, using the iPads in their studies had not had any noticeable impact on their digital literacy.

3.2. iPad Use in Studies

The students were asked to respond to 14 statements relating directly to their use of the iPad and their studies, stating how much they agree, or disagree, with each (Figure 4).

In 15/16, there are significant increases in the weighted average between semester 1 and semester 2 for several of the questions, most notably an increase in the weighted average of 0.38 for 'I feel better connected to my fellow students because of my iPad' and 0.31 for 'My iPad helps me communicate more effectively.'

All the students who took part in the group interviews reported using Facebook Messenger on their iPads to arrange group work, ask questions about course content and assignments, and for sharing resources. AIrdrop was also made use of for sharing files. Despite all students at the University having Office365 accounts and access to OneDrive, few reported this as a method of storing and sharing files.

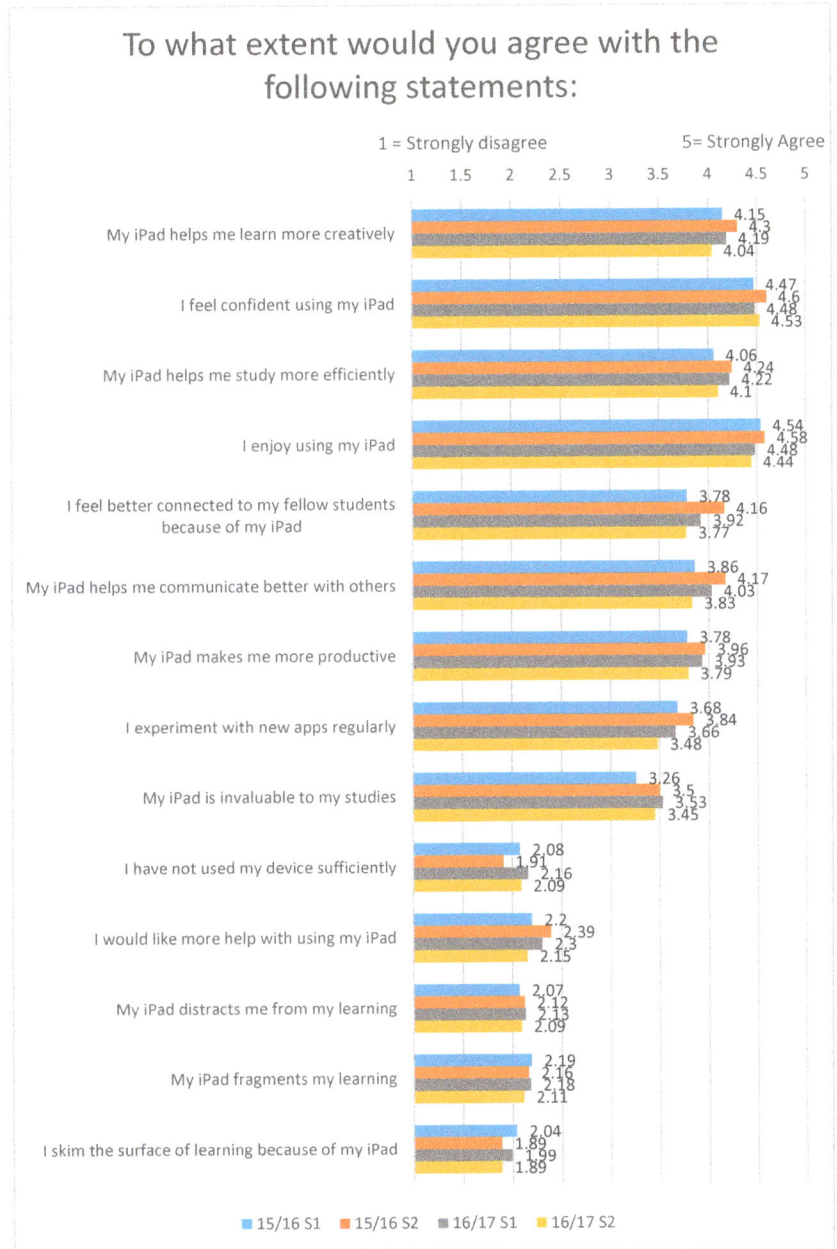

Figure 4. Questions relating to the use of iPads in studies.

In 15/16, smaller increases were seen for all the questions, with one exception, implying that, as the students become more accustomed to using the devices, they are finding them more beneficial. It is unclear why more help is wanted with using their iPads in semester 2 over semester 1, although this could be due to them becoming aware of new apps and/or functionality and wanting assistance with a particular aspect of device use. This is especially likely, due to the 0.13 increase for 'I feel confident using my iPad.'

The results for 16/17 differ to those of 15/16 and in many cases, demonstrate a downward trend in how the devices are being used, most notably a reduction in the weighted average of 0.20 for 'My iPad helps me communicate better with others' and 0.18 for 'I experiment with new apps regularly.' There is a decrease of 0.15 for both 'My iPad helps me learn more creatively' and 'I feel better connected to my fellow students because of my iPad' and a similar reduction for My iPad makes me more productive' (decrease of 0.14). These decreases come in spite of the students reporting increased confidence in using the devices (increase of 0.07) and wanting less help in using them (decrease of 0.15).

Prior device ownership is comparable between the two years, as are perceptions of digital literacy (variance of 0.04), and lecture observations revealed no significant changes in practice. As such, it is unclear as to why the students in 16/17 appear to find the devices of less benefit, although it is possible that staff may not be making as regular use of the iPads as the observations imply.

3.3. Technology Use in Studies

Students were asked to respond to eight statements relating to their use of technology in their studies, stating how much they agree, or disagree with each (Figure 5).

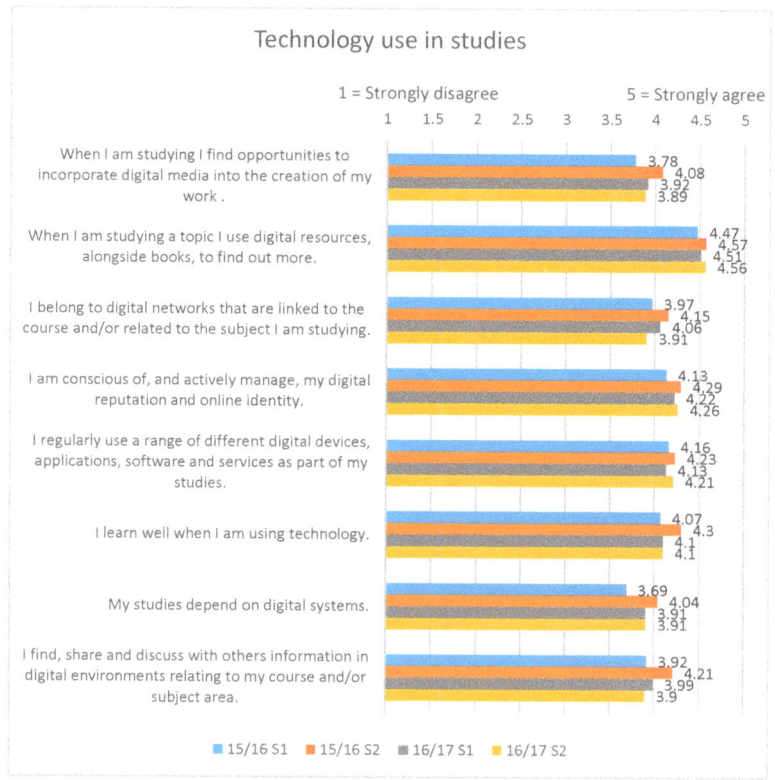

Figure 5. Technology use in studies.

As with the previous set of questions, there are some significant increases in the weighted averages between the semesters for 15/16. Most notable among these is an increase of 0.35 for 'My studies depend on digital systems,' perhaps indicating that by this point in the academic year the use of the iPads has been fully integrated into their studies.

Other significant increases include a rise of 0.30 for 'When I am studying I find opportunities to incorporate digital media into the creation of my work.' The group interviews and lecture observations have shown that the students are making use of the iPad's camera, taking short videos and still images to supplement typed or written notes. In the case of Primary Education students, these digital artefacts are often then being used in the portfolio they are required to keep. The 0.29 increase for 'I find, share and discuss with other information in digital environments relating to my course and/or subject area' is likely to relate to the aforementioned use of Facebook Messenger and file sharing tools, such as Airdrop.

The 16/17 results are much more mixed with some smaller increases in weighted average, some small decreases and some remaining unchanged. The most significant change is a decrease in the weighted average of 0.15 for the question 'I belong to digital networks that are linked to the course and/or related to the subject I am studying,' perhaps indicating a lack of time, or willingness, to engage with others in their subject area as their degree progresses and their studies become intense.

3.4. JISC Digital Experience Tracker

In 2017 the University took part in the JISC digital experience tracker. While the surveys undertaken as part of the iPilot demonstrate changes in perception and behavior over time, the data from the JISC digital experience tracker make it possible to compare the answers of iPilot and non-iPilot students against the national average. It should be noted that this survey took place during semester 2 of 16/17 and as such no data exists for the previous three semesters.

Figure 6 shows the percentage of students who reported never conducting certain digital behaviors and demonstrates that the iPilot students are more likely than non-iPilot students, and the national average, to undertake certain activities. In particular, the iPilot students are much more likely than the national average to 'access learning on the move,' implying that their iPads allow them to be more flexible in when and where they learn.

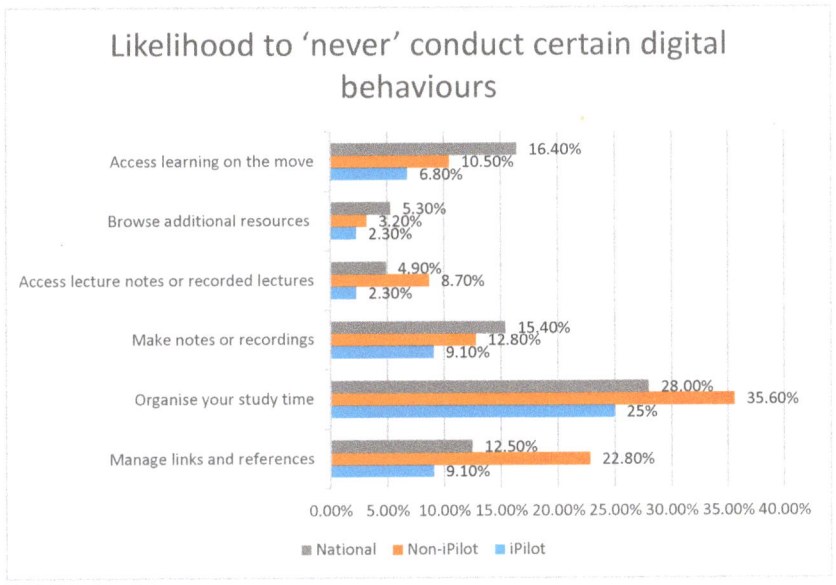

Figure 6. Likelihood to 'never' conduct certain digital behaviors.

4. Discussion

Overall, the results of this study showed that providing students with iPads and having the device's use embedded into the delivery of classroom activities has had a positive impact on students' perceptions of their own digital capabilities.

This is especially clear in the data from 15/16 which shows an increase in certain digital behaviors, and opinions relating to technology use in studies. This demonstrates that the more the students are making use of the devices in the classroom, the more opportunities they are discovering for utilizing technology in their learning, and the more vital that technology is becoming to their studies. This shows that the students clearly believe that using the iPads is having a positive effect on their digital capability. The free-text comments from the surveys relating to digital literacy do appear to suggest that the use of the devices has the most benefit for those students who do not already class themselves as very digitally capable, suggesting that those students who are on the higher end of this scale are operating above the level of the tasks undertaken. Future studies may find it beneficial to see whether there is any correlation between initial perceptions of digital capability and growth over time in these perceptions.

The 16/17 data are more troubling as it displays a reduction between semester 1 and semester 2 in student opinions relating to the iPads, technology and their studies. While this is not the case for all of the questions, enough display a downward trend to suggest that something had changed, despite lecture observations indicating that this was not the case. As alluded to earlier in this paper, tutors may have been making more of a 'show' in using the devices while they were being observed, as they were given at least a week's notice prior to the observation taking place. It is possible that by the final semester of the project the initial enthusiasm that staff displayed for using the devices had waned with time-pressures preventing staff from designing appropriate activities. This is supported by some comments from the group interviews and free-text comments from the surveys that indicate that the devices were not being used as often as some students expected or wanted.

Due to the rapid changes that technology tends to undergo, it is possible that changes to iOS (the operating system) could have contributed to the decline in use between semester 1 and 2 in 16/17 by removing or changing familiar functionality. Version 10 of iOS was released two weeks prior to the students receiving their iPad mini 2s and saw a number of minor updates during the academic year with version 10.3.1 being the final version that the students would have had access to during semester 2. However, reviewing the patch notes [30] does not reveal any major changes that would contribute to a decline in use, and software changes were not raised as an issue in either the surveys or group interviews and so, this is unlikely to have contributed.

It is likely that staff levels of digital capability may also have affected the frequency of use and types of tasks undertaken. As the project was so large, it is unsurprising that tutors displayed varying levels of digital literacy, from tutors who had never held an iPad to those who were Apple Recognized Educators, or who specialized in digital pedagogy. Several tutors remarked that they felt uncomfortable making use of the devices in class as they perceived their own digital capabilities to be much lower than the students'. The same tutors expressed an understanding that it is vital for students to possess these digital skills, and that as academics, it is partly their job to help the students acquire them. However, despite showing a willingness to expand their digital skillset, these tutors reported not having the time to attend training or conduct independent research on how to embed the devices into the delivery of their classes. In contrast, some tutors displayed over-confidence in using the devices in their teaching, due to prior experience of using iPads in their personal lives. However, this did not always translate into effective use in the classroom and, as with any piece of technology, it must be remembered that being able to use an iPad does not automatically mean that a tutor will be able to use them appropriately in teaching.

The Technological Pedagogical Content Knowledge (TPACK) framework [31] indicates that the staff referred to above, while all displaying strong content knowledge (CK) and pedagogical knowledge (PK) do not have the required skills and knowledge to effectively integrate these with technology.

It is interesting that some staff members who reported high levels of digital capability, displaying technology knowledge (TK) and technology content knowledge (TCK), were unable to make use of the devices effectively in their teaching, indicating that barriers exist to them truly understanding how technology, pedagogy and content knowledge (TPACK) can, and should, interact. This will help shape future training on mobile devices that staff receive.

While work has already been undertaken to draw relationships between academics' views of education and technology and student usage [21], future studies may wish to consider this with a particular focus on the use of mobile devices.

In contrast to, and despite, the general downward trend in many of 16/17 results, the JISC data suggests that the use of the devices is having a positive impact on certain digital behaviors. While non-iPilot students at the institution were less likely than the national average to access learning on the move or browse additional resources, the iPilot students consistently scored higher than both other groups. While this could be attributed to the fact that they all own iPads, the high levels of prior ownership of both smartphones and laptops, imply that new behaviors might be being formed through the use of the devices in-class.

When discussing these results, it is important to remember that the iPads used for this project are merely a tool and in themselves, did not provide any benefit. As Higgins et al. articulately state, it is "the pedagogy of the application of technology in the classroom which is important: The how rather than the what." [32] (p. 3). It is, therefore, the ways in which the students have been making use of the iPads, both inside and outside of the classroom, which will have had an impact on their digital capability skills and not the devices themselves. Due to the number of academics and students involved in this project, it was not feasible to gather precise information surrounding the types of activities that were being undertaken, and this is one area in which this study is lacking. Anecdotal evidence suggests that research tasks resulting in small group presentations are more beneficial than others, such as the use of audience response tools, but not enough concrete information has been gathered to definitively make a statement. Future studies, where the types of activities undertaken by students are categorized to see whether certain tasks provide more of a benefit than others, would be beneficial and would help those colleagues who wish to design curricula with embedded mobile device use.

As this study focused on the use of the devices in the university classroom, staff perceptions of both technology and effective teaching student perspectives of their digital capabilities will undoubtedly have had an impact on how the iPads were used, and as such, the level of impact that their use had on student perceptions of digital capabilities. Previous studies have drawn correlations between student engagement in technology-rich classrooms and tutors that see the importance in developing student self-reliance [24], whereas others have found that some perceptions of how technology impacts learning are unlikely to lead to successful integrations [33]. Related future studies may wish to ascertain staff perceptions of both technology and effective teaching prior to better understand how these factors affect student digital capabilities.

As a large-scale, cross-faculty initiative, where individuals had varying levels of experience of using technology, and tutors displayed differing teaching practices, within teams and across the institution, gathering detailed and granular data regarding device usage, and staff and student views, proved difficult. Future studies may wish to focus on a single discipline with a smaller number of staff and students as this may prove easier to monitor. Smaller studies may find it beneficial to focus on gathering qualitative rather than quantitative data, as the author believes that this may prove to be the richest source of information regarding opinions and device usage.

funding: This research was internally funded and received no external funding.

Conflicts of Interest: The author declares no conflict of interest. The funders had no role in the design of the study; in the collection, analyses, or interpretation of data; in the writing of the manuscript, and in the decision to publish the results.

References

1. JISC (Joint Information Systems Committee). Digital Capability and Employability. Available online: https://www.jisc.ac.uk/guides/designing-learning-and-assessment-in-a-digital-age/digital-capability-and-employability (accessed on 30 May 2018).
2. Masterman, L. From Digital Literacy to Digital Capabilities. Available online: https://blogs.it.ox.ac.uk/acit-news/2016/05/18/dig-lit-and-dig-cap/ (accessed on 29 May 2018).
3. Prensky, M. Digital Natives, Digital Immigrants Part 1. *Horiz. J. Serv. Manag.* **2001**, *9*, 245–267. [CrossRef]
4. Bennet, S.; Maton, K.; Kervin, L. The 'digital natives' debate: A critical review of the evidence. *Br. J. Educ. Technol.* **2008**, *39*, 775–786. [CrossRef]
5. Bullen, M.; Morgan, T.; Qayyum, A. Digital Learners in Higher Education: Generation is Not the Issue. *Can. J. Learn. Teach.* **2011**, *37*. Available online: https://www.cjlt.ca/index.php/cjlt/article/view/26364 (accessed on 4 July 2018). [CrossRef]
6. Jones, C.; Shao, B. The Net Generation and Digital Natives. Available online: https://www.heacademy.ac.uk/system/files/next-generation-and-digital-natives.pdf (accessed on 4 July 2018).
7. JISC (Joint Information Systems Committee). Developing Students' Digital Literacy. Available online: https://www.jisc.ac.uk/guides/developing-students-digital-literacy (accessed on 29 May 2018).
8. JISC (Joint Information Systems Committee). Building Digital Capabilities: The Six Elements Defined. Available online: http://repository.jisc.ac.uk/6611/1/JFL0066F_DIGIGAP_MOD_IND_FRAME.PDF (accessed on 30 May 2018).
9. JISC (Joint Information Systems Committee). Developing Organisational Approaches to Digital Capability. Available online: https://www.jisc.ac.uk/guides/developing-organisational-approaches-to-digital-capability (accessed on 29 May 2018).
10. JISC (Joint Information Systems Committee). JISC Building Digital Capability Blog. Available online: https://digitalcapability.jiscinvolve.org/wp/digital-capability-discovery-tool/ (accessed on 29 May 2018).
11. Austen, L.; Parkin, H.; Jones-Devitt, S.; McDonald, K.; Irwin, B. *Digital Capability and Teaching Excellence: An Integrative Review Exploring What Infrastructure and Strategies are Necessary to Support Effective Use of Technology Enabled Learning (TEL)*; Quality Assurance Agency for Higher Education: Gloucester, UK, 2016.
12. Lea, M.; Jones, S. Digital Literacies in higher education exploring textual and technological practice. *Stud. High. Educ.* **2011**, *36*, 377–393. [CrossRef]
13. Ofcom. Adults' Media Use and Attitudes, Report 2017. Available online: https://www.ofcom.org.uk/__data/assets/pdf_file/0020/102755/adults-media-use-attitudes-2017.pdf (accessed on 31 May 2018).
14. Statista. Global Apple iPad Sales from 3rd Fiscal Quarter of 2010 to 2nd Fiscal Quarter of 2018. Available online: https://www.statista.com/statistics/269915/global-apple-ipad-sales-since-q3-2010/ (accessed on 31 May 2018).
15. Manuguerra, M.; Petocz, P. Promoting student engagement by integrating new technology into tertiary education: The role of the iPad. *Asian Soc. Sci.* **2011**, *7*, 61–65. [CrossRef]
16. Yong Tay, H. Longitudinal study on impact of iPad use on teaching and learning. *Cogent Educ.* **2016**, *45*, 1–22.
17. UCISA. Mobile learning: How Mobile Technologies Can Enhance the Learning Experience. Available online: https://www.ucisa.ac.uk/publications/effective_use (accessed on 31 May 2018).
18. Morrone, A.; Gosney, J.; Engel, S. *Empowering Students and Instructors: Reflections on the Effectiveness of iPads for Teaching and Learning*; Educause: Louisville, CO, USA, 2012.
19. Dimer, T.; Fernandez, E.; Streepey, J. Student perceptions of classroom engagement and learning using iPads. *J. Teach. Learn. Technol.* **2012**, *1*, 13–25.
20. Nguyen, L.; Barton, S.; Nguyen, L. iPads in higher education—hype and hope. *Br. J. Educ. Technol.* **2015**, *46*, 190–203. [CrossRef]
21. Aiyegbayo, O. How and why academics do and do not use iPads for academic teaching? *Br. J. Educ. Technol.* **2015**, *46*, 1324–1332. [CrossRef]
22. Morrison, M.; Leah, J.; Harvey, F.; Masters, C. Embedding the iPad as a learning and teaching tool: A case study of staff and student perspectives in a management school. In *iPads in Higher Education*; Souleles, N., Pillar, C., Eds.; Cambridge Scholars Publishing: Newcastle, UK, 2015; pp. 39–59.
23. Gregory, M.; Lodge, J. Academic workload: The silent barrier to the implementation of technology-enhanced learning strategies in higher education. *Distance Educ.* **2015**, 210–230. [CrossRef]

24. Gebre, E.; Saroyan, A.; Bracewell, R. Students' engagement in technology rich classrooms and its relationship to professors' conceptions of effective teaching. *Br. J. Educ. Technol.* **2014**, *45*, 83–96. [CrossRef]

25. Hyland, P.; Jessop, T.; El-Hakim, Y.; Adams, J.; Barlow, A.; Morgan, G.; Shepherd, C. FASTECH Project Final Evaluation Report. JISC. Available online: http://jiscdesignstudio.pbworks.com/w/page/49920023/Assessment%20and%20Feedback%20Programme (accessed on 30 May 2018).

26. UOW Mobile Device Scheme. Available online: https://uowmobiledevicescheme.wordpress.com/about/ (accessed on 30 May 2018).

27. Elphick, M.; Sims, S. Reflections on Encouraging the Use of Mobile Devices through Staff-Student Partnership. *J. Educ. Innov. Partnersh. Chang.* **2017**, *3*, 5. Available online: https://journals.gre.ac.uk/index.php/studentchangeagents/article/view/573 (accessed on 31 May 2018). [CrossRef]

28. JISC. Student Digital Experience Tracker. Available online: https://www.jisc.ac.uk/rd/projects/student-digital-experience-tracker (accessed on 30 May 2018).

29. JISC (Joint Information Systems Committee). Developing Digital Literacies. Available online: https://www.jisc.ac.uk/guides/developing-digital-literacies (accessed on 30 May 2018).

30. Apple. Download iOS 10.0–iOS 10.3.3 Information. Available online: https://support.apple.com/kb/DL1893?locale=en_US (accessed on 4 July 2018).

31. Koehler, M.; Mishra, P. What is Technological Pedagogical Content Knowledge? *Contemp. Issues Technol. Teach. Educ.* **2009**, *9*, 60–70. [CrossRef]

32. Higgins, S.; Xiao, Z.; Katsipataki, M. The Impact of Digital Technology on Learning: A Summary for the Education Endowment Foundation. Available online: https://educationendowmentfoundation.org.uk/public/files/Publications/The_Impact_of_Digital_Technologies_on_Learning_(2012).pdf (accessed on 30 May 2018).

33. Cope, C.; Ward, P. Integrating learning technology into classrooms: The importance of teachers' perceptions. *J. Educ. Technol. Soc.* **2002**, *5*, 67–74.

education sciences

Article

The Effects of Using Mobile Devices on Student Achievement in Language Learning: A Meta-Analysis

Kyunghwa Cho [1], Sungwoong Lee [2], Min-Ho Joo [3,*] and Betsy Jane Becker [4]

[1]   Educational Psychology and Learning Systems, College of Education, Florida State University,
     1114 W. Call St., Tallahassee, FL 32306, USA; ckh1745@gmail.com
[2]   Instructional Design and Technology, The Teachers College, Emporia State University, 328I, 1 Kellogg Circle,
     Emporia, KS 66801, USA; slee42@emporia.edu
[3]   Department of Educational Technology, College of Education, Konkuk University, 120 Neungdong-ro,
     Gwangjin-gu, Seoul 05029, Korea
[4]   Educational Psychology and Learning Systems, College of Education, Florida State University,
     3210D Stone Building, 1114 W. Call St., Tallahassee, FL 32306, USA; bbecker@fsu.edu
*   Correspondence: minhojoo@konkuk.ac.kr

Received: 1 June 2018; Accepted: 16 July 2018; Published: 23 July 2018

Abstract: The use of mobile technologies has recently received great attention in language learning. Most research evaluates the effects of employing mobile devices in language learning and explores the design of mobile-learning interventions that can maximize the benefits of new technologies. However, it is still unclear whether the use of mobile devices in language learning is more effective than other instructional approaches. It is also not clear whether the effects of mobile-device use vary in different settings. Our meta-analysis will explore these questions about mobile technology use in language learning. Based on the specific inclusion and exclusion criteria, 22 d-type effect sizes from 20 studies were calculated for the meta-analysis. We adopted the random-effects model, and the estimated average effect was 0.51 ($se = 0.10$). This is a moderate positive overall effect of using mobile devices on language acquisition and language-learning achievement. Moderator analyses under the mixed-effects model examined six features; effects varied significantly only by test type and source of the study. The overall effect and the effects of these moderators of mobile-device use on achievement in language learning are discussed.

Keywords: mobile device; m-learning; language learning; achievement; mobile technologies; meta-analysis; instructional approaches

1. Introduction

With the rapid growth of mobile technologies as well as the explosion in the number of educational applications and mobile devices, a large number of studies have been conducted about the use of mobile devices in education [1–4]. Widespread ownership of mobile devices has cued researchers to pay attention to mobile devices as potential media to deliver learning content [5–7], and to consider how to use mobile devices as pedagogical support tools [8,9]. Educators have not only begun to use mobile technologies in formal classroom settings but have also integrated such technologies into informal education settings in daily life [7,9].

Language learning is one area in which the use of mobile technologies has been well researched [10]. Previous studies have identified advantages of mobile devices including their portability, versatility of features, connectivity, and individuality [6,11,12]. Their portability, combined with the pervasive presence of mobile devices in daily life, enables learners to use handheld devices anytime they want [9,13–15]. In addition, research on language learning can be conducted not only in formal classrooms but also in informal settings such as during language use at home and in social communication. Therefore, language learning is a domain in which mobile devices can play an important role in educational activities [1,16,17].

1.1. Definition of Mobile Learning

Mobile devices such as smartphones and tablets are becoming ubiquitous. Unlike other forms of e-learning that deliver educational content via the internet, mobile learning or m-learning has one certain benefit: learner mobility [18–23]. Mobile learning combines student support tools from e-learning with mobile technology, thus allowing access to educational content or information without the limitations of physical location or time [9]. That is, mobile learning can be defined as any sort of learning in which content or facilitated educational activities are delivered using mobile technologies as mediating tools, whenever and wherever the learner desires [9].

1.2. Trends in Mobile Learning in Education

Mobile learning is increasingly being recognized as a potential learning environment in education [1,7]. The adoption of mobile technologies is rapidly expanding in higher education, in primary and secondary schools, and in training contexts [9]. According to a report by the Pew Research Center [24], 73% of Advanced Placement and National Writing Project teachers reported that they and/or their students used cell phones for educational purposes in the classroom or when they worked on assignments. In addition, 45% of teachers and students reported use of e-readers, and 43% of teachers or students indicated use of tablet computers in the classroom or for assignments.

Why do both teachers and students rely on mobile technologies? Three potential answers are (1) mobile phones are nearly always present in daily life, (2) smartphones can be used as hand-held computers to support learning activities with integrated technologies such as voice recorder/player, camera/camcorder, web browser, and personal computing [23], and (3) numerous mobile applications are being developed for educational activities. With these features of mobile devices and their potential capabilities as pedagogical support tools, the landscape of technology-supported learning highlights mobile learning as a critical emerging area [23,25,26]. According to reviews of trends in mobile-learning research [4,7], studies of mobile learning have examined a diversity of disciplines including the humanities, social sciences, health sciences, and natural sciences. Language and linguistics, a sub-discipline of the humanities, has the largest number of studies on mobile learning. In addition, five reviews [1,4,7,18,19] have synthesized general mobile-learning trends. Wu et al. [4] (2012) noted that, from 2003 to 2010, many researchers focused on the effectiveness of mobile learning (i.e., 58% of mobile-learning studies). These reviews reported valuable information on how different types of mobile-device use and mobile-device-based learning environments hold benefits for other mobile-learning settings. In addition, those aforementioned reviews represented the overall research trends related to the use of mobile technology in the field of education.

1.3. Mobile-Assisted Language Learning

Researchers in language learning and linguistics have attempted to use technology-supported learning to enhance learning outcomes and learner performance in numerous ways [7,14,15,27,28]. Mobile-Assisted Language Learning (MALL) is a technology-supported approach to language learning, which focuses on acquisition of linguistic knowledge and skills as well as providing assistance with communication using emerging mobile technology [29].

The use of mobile technologies has recently received great attention in language learning [4,9,14,30,31]. Language learning is defined as the process of development in language ability. For example, current mobile-learning trends indicate that the largest numbers of studies on mobile learning have focused on language and linguistic disciplines [4]. In MALL studies, scholars evaluate the effects of employing mobile devices in language learning and explore the design of mobile-learning interventions that can maximize the benefits of new technologies [14,32,33].

A variety of language skills may be considered under the umbrella of language learning. One of course is the learning of a new language. Learning a language requires one to learn vocabulary words, to recognize them when listening and reading, and to pronounce them properly. As well, one needs to understand and be able to independently produce the grammatical structures of the language being learned [34]. More mundane and concrete skills such as spelling and using proper punctuation are also parts of language learning. However, these skills are not only needed when learning a second language, they are relevant to one's first-language skill improvement as well. Learning more words, and more complex words, is an important part of being an advanced reader [16]. Reading itself is a language skill [35,36].

Some of these component skills in language learning are thought to be particularly suitable to mobile learning. Vocabulary accumulation [37] and pronunciation [38] appear ideally suited for the mobile-learning context.

However, it is still unclear whether the use of mobile devices in language learning is more effective than other instructional approaches such as language learning with computers or print-based materials. It is also not clear whether the effects of mobile-device use vary in different settings. Our meta-analysis will explore these questions about mobile-technology use in language learning.

In this review, we synthesize the results of experimental studies that measure the effects of using mobile devices on language learning. We investigate the effects of using mobile devices in language learning using the methods of meta-analysis. We offer a systematic review and synthesize the findings of relevant documents (e.g., published articles, dissertations, reports, etc.) from the language-learning and linguistics disciplines. Specifically, the goal of our meta-analysis is to answer the following two research questions:

Research question 1. What is the average effect of using mobile devices on language learning?

Research question 2. How do the effects of using mobile devices vary when language achievement is measured in different research settings and contexts, at different school levels, in different types of study, and for different target language-learning skills, types of test, and target language learners?

2. Methods

2.1. Data Search Strategy and Study Selection

A systematic literature search was conducted to explore relevant publications on MALL. Electronic databases including ERIC, EBSCOhost (Academic Search Complete), PsycINFO, JSTOR, and ProQuest Dissertations & Theses were used for the literature search. The key words ("language learning" AND "achievement") AND ("mobile" OR "m-learning") were used as distinct search terms. We located 337 articles in ERIC and 776 articles in EBSCOhost. In addition, we found 264 articles from PsycINFO and 1345 articles from JSTOR. For unpublished studies, ProQuest Dissertations & Theses was used, and 147 studies were found (see Figure 1). The research results were limited to have publication dates between 2005 and 2017 because most mobile learning studies have been conducted since 2005. We found no study results from conference papers and books suitable for inclusion in our meta-analysis.

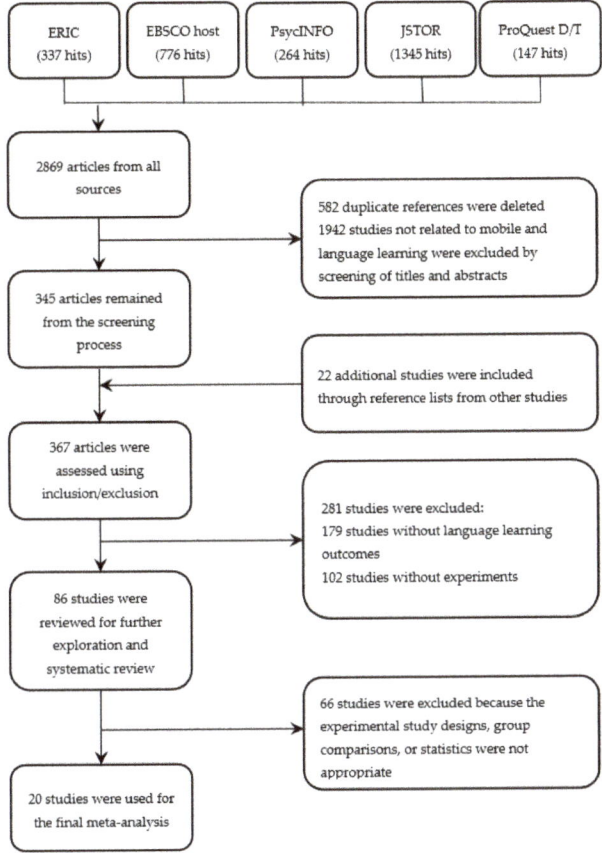

Figure 1. Flow chart of the literature search.

2.2. Inclusion and Exclusion Rules

The results of the literature search and study exclusions were shown in Figure 1. A total of 2869 articles was found after conducting the first exploratory searches through the electronic databases. After a series of screening decisions, 345 potentially relevant articles were identified. The following criteria were used for inclusion of the studies: the study had (1) included mobile learning as a treatment plus some control condition, (2) used an experimental design to compare mobile learning and some other intervention, (3) included educational activities delivered via mobile devices, (4) included a clear description of participants, and (5) provided sufficient statistical information to allow computation of *d*-type effect sizes. In addition, collected sources were excluded if the studies (1) were not related to mobile learning and language-learning, (2) did not measure language learning achievement as a learning outcome, (3) were published before 2005, or (4) showed unusually large effect sizes as outliers. Based on the inclusion and exclusion criteria, 367 articles were excluded, and 86 studies were retained for further exploration and coding. Finally, 20 studies remained for the meta-analysis.

2.3. Data Evaluation

A total of 20 studies provided 22 effect sizes. A list of studies and coded features is presented in Table 1. The coded features included: (1) participant information, (2) treatment and setting characteristics, and (3) statistics used, including sample size, means, and standard deviations.

Table 1. List of selected studies with key features.

Author(s)	d	N	School Level	Source of Study	Context of Study	Target Language Learning Skill	Type of Test	Target Language-Learner
Ali, Segaran & Hoe [39] (2015)	0.32	60	Post-secondary	Journal	Formal	Pronunciation	Researcher-made scale	ESL
Basogh, & Akdemir [40] (2010)	0.58	58	Post-secondary	Journal	Formal	Vocabulary	Researcher-made scale	ESL
Billings & Mathison [41] (2012)	0.46	242	Primary	Journal	Informal	Vocabulary	Researcher-made scale	ESL
Frown [35] (2008)	−0.27	63	Secondary	Dissertation	Formal	Vocabulary	Commercial standardized test	EFL
Elfeky & Masadeh [13] (2016)	1.57	75	Post-secondary	Journal	Formal	Language arts	Researcher-made scale	ESL
Fishburn [36] (2008)	0.45	292	Primary	Dissertation	Formal	Reading	Researcher-made scale	EFL
Hsu, Hwang & Chang [11] (2013)	0.64	108	Secondary	Journal	Formal	Reading	Commercial standardized test	ESL
Ketyi [42] (2015)	0.58	94	Post-secondary	Journal	Formal	Language arts	Researcher-made scale	ESL
Khrisat & Mahmoud [43] (2013)	0.17	40	Post-secondary	Journal	Informal	Language arts	Researcher-made scale	ESL
Kordo et al. [44] (2012)	0.26	88	Post-secondary	Journal	Formal	Language arts	Commercial standardized test	ESL
Lu [28] (2008)	0.96	30	Secondary	Journal	Formal	Vocabulary	Researcher-made scale	ESL
Mellati & Khademi [45] (2015)	1.29	68	Post-secondary	Journal	Informal	Language arts	Researcher-made scale	ESL
Sandberg, Maris & de Geus [15] (2011)	0.28	75	Primary	Journal	Formal	Vocabulary	Researcher-made scale	ESL
Saran, Seferoglu & Cagiltay [38] (2009)	1.37	24	Primary	Journal	Formal	Pronunciation	Researcher-made scale	ESL
Saran, Seferoglu & Cagiltay [46] (2012)	1.08	53	Primary	Journal	Formal	Vocabulary	Researcher-made scale	ESL
Walters [47] (2012)	0.06	414	Primary	Dissertation	Formal	Reading, Language arts	Commercial standardized test	ESL
	−0.02	67						
Wang [3] (2017)	0.33	63	Post-secondary	Journal	Formal	Reading	Commercial standardized test	ESL
	−0.06	66						
Wu & Huang [48] (2017)	0.90	94	Post-secondary	Journal	Formal	Vocabulary	Researcher-made scale	ESL
Yang, Hwang, Hung & Tseng [16] (2013)	0.62	92	Primary	Journal	Formal	Reading	Researcher-made scale	ESL
Zhang, Song & Burston [37] (2011)	0.62	78	Post-secondary	Journal	Informal	Vocabulary	Commercial standardized test	ESL

Note. ESL = English as a second language learner; EFL = English as a first language learner.

2.3.1. Initial Coding

The first coding category, study information, included school level, total sample size, and publication type. Treatment and setting characteristics included features such as the context of the study, type of mobile device, intervention components, and representation of content. In addition to these two major categories, information to calculate effect sizes was collected. Because the main research questions were related to the effects of mobile-device use versus other conventional learning interventions, means and standard deviations or other statistics were used to compute *d*-type effect sizes; these are listed in Table 1.

2.3.2. Moderators

Six potential moderator variables—school level, source of study, context of study, target language-learning skill, type of test, and target language learner–were identified as shown in Table 1. School level was divided into three categories: (1) primary, (2) secondary, and (3) post-secondary. Source of study classified the publication outlet of the research, as either (1) journal or (2) dissertation. Context of study identified whether the research was conducted in a formal or informal learning environment. Formal learning was defined as the act of acquiring knowledge or skills in highly structured, classroom-based, or institutionalized settings [49,50]. Thus, formal learning in this review referred to the use of mobile devices in structured classroom instruction, or during homework. Informal learning was intentional but not highly structured [50]. Here, informal learning referred to the use of mobile devices for learning in social activities or field trips which were not part of classroom-based instruction. Target language-learning skill was divided into four categories: (1) vocabulary, (2) pronunciation, (3) reading, and (4) language arts. Type of test had two categories: (1) commercial standardized tests and (2) researcher-made scales which were developed for each specific study. Target language learner in this review represented the focus group for English language learning: (1) English as a Second Language (ESL) learner group vs. (2) English as a First Language (EFL) learner group.

2.4. Extraction and Calculation of Effect Sizes

Twenty-two effect sizes were extracted from the 20 studies that remained after applying the inclusion/exclusion rules. If a study included results of multiple experiments or subgroups, the effect sizes were calculated separately for each sample. For example, Wang [3] studied the effects of using mobile devices on comprehensive reading with three different majors in post-secondary school: business administration, information management, and tourism management. In this case, three independent effect sizes were extracted. On the other hand, multiple outcomes from a study were averaged due to the dependency that exists when examining the same participants repeatedly. To avoid the overestimation of variance when the dependency of effect sizes occurred, the robust variance estimation (RVE) method [51] was applied to calculate the corresponding variances of effect sizes.

Our main research questions related to the effects of mobile devices versus those of other learning interventions. Thus, effect sizes (*d*) were obtained by calculating the difference between the means of the experimental (mobile) and control (other treatment) groups, divided by the pooled standard deviation as shown in Equation (1):

$$
\begin{aligned}
d &= \frac{\overline{X}_T - \overline{X}_C}{S_P} \times c\,(m-1), \\
S_P &= \sqrt{\frac{(n^T-1)S_T^2 + (n^C-1)S_C^2}{(n^T-1)+(n^C-1)}}, \\
c\,(m) &= 1 - \frac{3}{4m-1}
\end{aligned}
\tag{1}
$$

Also, n^T and n^C are the sample sizes for the mobile learning and control groups, respectively, and $m = n^T + n^C - 2$.

The variance of the effect size was calculated using

$$Var(d) = v = \frac{n^T + n^C}{n^T n^C} + \frac{d^2}{2(n^T + n^C)} \tag{2}$$

In the case of different study designs or analyses of the primary studies, such as analysis of covariance, the effect size (*d*) was calculated by using the adjusted means in the numerator, assuming the adjustments were reasonable, and using the pooled unadjusted standard deviation for the calculation [52].

2.5. Coding and Effect Size Reliabilities

All 22 effect sizes from 20 studies and six moderators were coded independently at least twice by three of the authors, and then their results were compared to assess inter-coder reliability. For effect sizes, the reliability was calculated as a Pearson correlation. The reliabilities of other key variables were calculated using the proportion of agreement. All disagreements were discussed until any discrepancies were fully resolved. The reliabilities of initial codes for the effect sizes and moderators are shown in Table 2.

Table 2. Inter-coder reliability.

	n	*d*	School Level	Source of Study	Context of Study	Target Language Learning Skill	Type of Test	Target Language-Learner
Reliability	0.95	0.78	1	1	0.86	0.92	1	1

2.6. Data Analysis

2.6.1. Applications Used for the Meta-Analysis

To assess the heterogeneity of our effect sizes and potential for publication bias, we drew confidence interval (CI) plots and the funnel plot [53], using Excel and R. To explore possible moderators for the effect size of the impact of mobile devices on language learning, SPSS macros developed by David Wilson, including MeanES and MetaF, were used to compute Q statistics including Q_B (i.e., the Q value for testing between groups differences) and Q_W (i.e., the Q value for remaining within groups variability). These macros were available at http://mason.gmu.edu/~dwilsonb/ma.html.

2.6.2. Publication Bias

Publication bias is defined as "the state of affairs when published research on a topic is systematically unrepresentative of the population of completed studies on that topic" [53] (p. 61). Rothstein and Dickersin [54] listed several sources of publication bias, including editorial policies, unpublished or delayed reports of statistically non-significant studies, and over-representation of large results for overall effect size due to sample size. Rothstein and Dickersin argued that publication bias was a potential threat to the validity of meta-analytic results. In the current review, the funnel plot, trim-and-fill method, and Egger's test were employed for evaluating publication bias. In the funnel plot, effects from larger more precise studies appear at the top of the plot, whereas those from smaller, less precise studies appear more dispersed at the bottom of the graph. If publication bias does not exist and the effects are from a single population, the effects will be distributed symmetrically and form the shape of an upside-down funnel. The plot typically will be skewed to one side in the presence of publication bias [53]. The trim-and-fill method is used to estimate the number of studies missing from a meta-analysis in a funnel plot and to adjust the mean accordingly. Egger's test checks for asymmetry of the funnel plot; both it and the funnel plot are good indices for checking for publication bias.

2.6.3. Model Specification

Borenstein, Hedges, Higgins, and Rothstein [55] described two statistical models for meta-analysis: the fixed-effects model and the random-effects model. In the simplest fixed-effects model perspective, one true effect size exists for all studies, and all differences between effect sizes are assumed to be due to sampling error. The random-effects model consists of a common effect with two sources of variance: between studies variation and sampling error.

The effect sizes in this review were inspected to see whether they came from the same population. First, an overall homogeneity test was conducted using Hedges' formula for Q based on inverse variance weighting (using $w = 1/\text{Var}(d)$). Second, I-squared and the Birge ratio were computed, and CIs for the effect sizes [52] were plotted in order to assess the variability between studies.

When the homogeneity test verified that the effect sizes were not from a single homogeneous population, then it would be sensible to explore the variation in effects, to determine whether some of the between studies variance was explained by our moderator variables [52].

Based on both Q_B and Q_W statistics in our moderator analysis, we employed the random-effects model and the analysis-of-variance or ANOVA-like mixed-effects model. The weight was the inverse of the sum of the effect variance $\text{Var}(d_{ij})$ and the within-group random-effects variance, specifically.

$$w_i^M = \frac{1}{\text{Var}(d_{ij}) + V_j} \qquad (3)$$

for study i in group j.

2.6.4. Moderator Analysis

We considered six variables as moderators of effect size: school level, source of study, context of study, target language learning skill of study, type of test, and target language-learner. All these variables were categorical.

3. Results

3.1. Publication Bias Analysis

The funnel plot showing the effect-size standard error (on the vertical axis) versus effect size (on the horizontal axis) allowed us to assess potential publication bias and is shown in Figure 2. This asymmetrical funnel plot reflected some potential publication bias. The funnel plot showed more positive effects than negative ones; also several very large effects (above 2) were seen. The reference line showed the mean of the observed effects, which is 0.51.

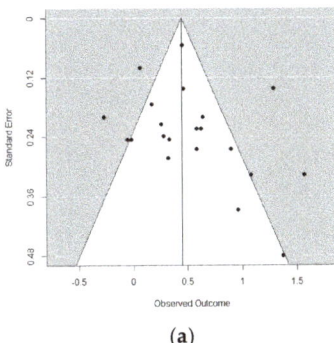
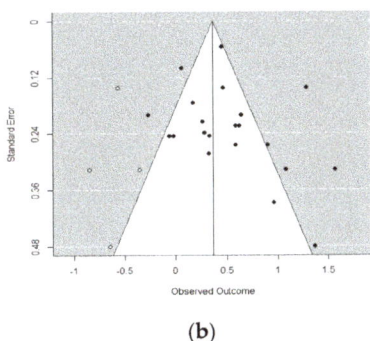

(a) (b)

Figure 2. Funnel plots. (**a**) Funnel plots for effect sizes in this meta-analysis (left); (**b**) Funnel plots adding possible missing effects as open circles (right).

We next conducted Egger's regression test for asymmetry [56]. Egger's test evaluates the intercept of the regression of the standard normal deviate of each effect on the precision, $1/Var$. The standard normal deviate was calculated as the effect size divided by the standard error of the effect size or $d/\sqrt{Var_i}$. This regression test for funnel-plot asymmetry under the mixed-effects meta-regression model with the predictor of standard error was not statistically significant with $z = 1.83$ at alpha level 0.05. Therefore, the intercept for this test suggested no evidence of funnel-plot asymmetry. In the funnel plot, most missing studies (i.e., the four estimated missing studies) were to the left of the mean. After applying the trim-and-fill method, the adjusted mean was decreased to $d = 0.36$, ($se = 0.03$) from the original overall effect size of $d = 0.51$, ($se = 0.10$) in Figure 2.

3.2. Overall Effect Size

As shown in the forest plot in Figure 3, no common effect size seemed evident given the wide array of the twenty-five confidence intervals. This result was consistent with heterogeneity of the effect-size data. The overall homogeneity test suggested that the data were not homogeneous ($Q = 103.27$, $df = 21$, $p < 0.05$). In addition, the values of Birge's ratio (4.92) and I-squared (79.66%) also supported the view that the effect sizes were not homogeneous. Based on the results of the homogeneity test, it was not reasonable to estimate a common effect. Any overall effect would represent an average of the set of population effect sizes. The next steps were to estimate the degree of heterogeneity of the effect sizes from different populations and to examine the effects of the moderator variables.

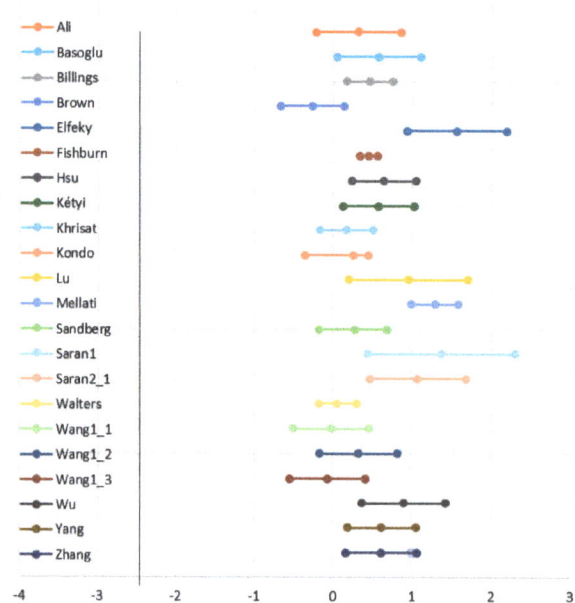

Figure 3. The confidence interval plot of effect sizes. The *x*-axis represents the standardized-mean-difference effect size (*d*) and the *y*-axis shows the names of the first authors of the primary studies.

Table 3 shows the overall weighted mean and homogeneity test for the 22 independent effect sizes. Because of the heterogeneity of effect sizes, we first proceeded with a random-effects model overall analysis. The overall mean effect size was strong ($d = 0.51$) with a random effects variance component of 0.10. This was used to estimate the interval within which 95% of all population effects might fall (assuming normality). This interval was from 0.32 to 0.70, indicating mobile learning was significantly more effective than the other interventions for language learning.

Table 3. Weighted mean effect sizes for mobile language-learning achievement under various conditions.

		Effect Size		95% CI		Test of Null	Test of Heterogeneity	
	k	*d*	*se*	*LL*	*UL*	*z*	Q_B	*df*
All studies	22	0.51	0.09	0.33	0.68	5.68		
School level							0.35	2
Elementary & kindergarten	7	0.52	0.16	0.20	0.84	3.18		
Secondary school	3	0.37	0.26	−0.14	1.41	1.41		
Undergraduate and beyond	12	0.54	0.13	0.29	0.79	4.24 *		
Source of study							4.07 *	1
Journal	19	0.59	0.10	0.40	0.79	5.94 *		
Dissertation	3	0.11	0.22	−0.32	0.54	0.50		
Context of study							0.49	1
Formal learning	18	0.54	0.10	0.34	0.74	5.26 *		
Informal learning	4	0.38	0.21	−0.03	0.79	1.84		
Target language-learning skill							1.41	3
Vocabulary	8	0.54	0.17	0.20	0.88	3.08 *		
Language arts	6	0.62	0.24	0.24	0.99	3.22 *		
Reading	6	0.34	0.19	−0.04	0.72	1.76		
Pronunciation	2	0.73	0.40	−0.05	1.51	1.82		
Type of test							9.18 *	1
Commercial standardized test	8	0.19	0.13	−0.07	0.45	1.46		
Researcher-made scale	14	0.70	0.10	0.49	0.90	6.70*		
Target language-learner							1.80	1
ESL	20	0.56	0.11	0.35	0.77	5.24 *		
EFL	2	0.12	0.31	−0.48	0.73	0.40		

Note. CI = confidence interval; LL = lower limit, UL = upper limit.* $p < 0.05$.

3.3. Moderator Variable Analysis

We next inspected the six potential moderators of our effect sizes. According to the ANOVA-like mixed-effects model with moderators (Table 4), only source of study and type of test were significant moderators. Table 4 shows the weighted mean effect sizes for language-learning achievement under various conditions.

Table 4. The results of moderator analyses with Q_B and Q_W.

	Effect Size			95% CI			
	d	*se*	*k*	*LL*	*UL*	Q_B	Q_W
School Level	0.51	0.09		0.33	0.69	0.35	22.74
Elementary & Kindergarten	0.52	0.16	7	0.20	0.84		5.10
Secondary School	0.37	0.26	3	−0.14	0.88		3.91
Post-secondary	0.54	0.13	12	0.29	0.79		13.73
Source of Study	0.51	0.09		0.33	0.69	4.07 *	20.49
Journal	0.59	0.10	19	0.40	0.79		18.71
Dissertation	0.11	0.22	3	−0.32	0.54		1.78
Context of Study	0.51	0.09		0.33	0.69	0.49	23.29
Formal Learning	0.54	0.10	18	0.34	0.74		22.61
Informal Learning	0.38	0.21	4	−0.03	0.79		0.68
Target Language Skill	0.52	0.10		0.31	0.72	1.41	17.79
Vocabulary	0.54	0.17	8	0.20	0.88		5.44
Language Arts	0.62	0.19	6	0.24	0.99		8.68
Reading	0.34	0.19	6	−0.04	0.72		2.03
Pronunciation	0.73	0.40	2	−0.05	1.51		1.65
Test Type	0.50	0.08		0.34	0.66	9.18 *	20.62
Commercial Standardized Test	0.19	0.13	8	−0.07	0.45		5.39
Researcher-made Scale	0.70	0.10	14	0.49	0.90		15.23
Type of Language-Learner	0.52	0.10		0.32	0.71	1.80	18.12
ESL	0.56	0.11	20	0.35	0.77		16.77
EFL	0.12	0.31	2	−0.48	0.73		1.35

Note. CI = confidence interval; LL = lower limit, UL = Upper limit.* $p < 0.05$.

3.3.1. School Level

We compared the effect sizes across school levels. As shown in Table 4, studies done in primary and post-secondary schools both showed significant detectable effect sizes, $d = 0.52$ ($se = 0.16$) and $d = 0.54$ ($se = 0.13$), respectively. Studies of learners in secondary school showed a mean effect size that was not significantly different from zero. However, because of high degrees of variation within each of the school levels, school level was not a moderator that could explain all the population variance in the effects ($Q_B = 0.35$, $p > 0.05$).

3.3.2. Source of Study

Studies in the current review were from two sources: journal articles and dissertations. A finding that larger effects were reported in journal articles led us to suspect publication bias may be at play. As shown in Table 4, mean effect sizes from journal articles were significantly larger than the mean effect sizes from dissertations ($Q_B = 4.07$, $p < 0.05$). Mobile-learning studies that were reported in journal articles also showed non-zero effects ($d = 0.59$, $se = 0.10$), whereas results based on dissertations showed virtually no effect with a mean of 0.11 ($se = 0.22$).

3.3.3. Context of Study

The context-of-study predictor included two categories: formal and informal learning. As shown in Table 4, mean effect sizes were significantly detectable from zero for the mobile-learning studies conducted in both formal-learning settings and informal-learning settings. The means of 0.54 ($se = 0.10$) and 0.38 ($se = 0.21$) represented moderate to large effects in both settings. However, the value of Q_B was not significant at $\alpha = 0.05$ ($Q_B = 0.49$). Therefore, we determined that the study context was not a moderator explaining the effect-size differences.

3.3.4. Target Language-Learning Skill

Four learning outcomes were examined in the mobile-learning studies we gathered: vocabulary, language arts, reading, and pronunciation. As shown in Table 4, learning outcomes for vocabulary, language arts, and pronunciation had strong positive effects. Only the reading learning outcome showed a weak effect. Thus, use of mobile devices appeared effective for language-learning achievement across most target language-learning skills. However, the value of Q_B was again not significant at $\alpha = 0.05$ ($Q_B = 1.41$, $p > 0.05$), so that the target language-learning skill predictor did not moderate the effects of mobile device use on language learning in this mixed-effects model.

3.3.5. Type of Test

The test-type predictor included two types of test: commercial standardized tests and researcher-made scales. The results demonstrated that mobile-learning outcomes that were measured with researcher-made scales were significantly different from those from the studies conducted with commercial standardized tests. Researcher-made scales showed much higher effect sizes ($d = 0.70$, $se = 0.10$) than standardized commercial tests ($d = 0.19$, $se = 0.13$).

3.3.6. Target Language Learner

The target language-learner predictor includes two types of student who participated in the studies: ESL and EFL. In this review, nearly all the studies in language-learning achievement were conducted with English as second language learners, except for two studies. In addition, larger effects were reported for ESL learners than for EFL learners. Mobile-learning studies which focused on ESL also showed non-zero effects ($d = 0.56$, $se = 0.11$), whereas results for EFL showed virtually no effect with a mean of 0.12 ($se = 0.31$). However, due to the very great uncertainty associated with the EFL mean, the target participant predictor was not a significant moderator, with Q_B value of 1.80 ($p > 0.05$).

4. Discussion

This study synthesized 22 effect sizes from 20 studies and investigated the effects of using mobile devices on students' achievement in language learning. Specifically, language-learning achievement was examined in different research settings and circumstances, including different school levels and study contexts. Also, studies varied in their target language-learning skills, type of tests used, and target language-learner populations. Results included were both published and unpublished (i.e., from dissertations).

4.1. Overall Effects of Using Mobile Devices on Achievement in Language Learning

The result of a medium sized overall positive effect of using mobile devices on language acquisition and language-learning achievement confirmed that the use of mobile devices could facilitate language learning. These results were consistent with other research findings regarding the effects of mobile devices on subsequent language-learning skills, such as vocabulary [27,28,37,57] and general language acquisition [30,58]. In addition, the result connected with recent systematic reviews and meta-analyses [2,7,59].

4.2. The Effects of Using Mobile Devices under Various Conditions

School Level. Finding large effect sizes for using mobile devices in all school levels indicated employing mobile devices with students can influence language acquisition and achievement.

Context of Study. Both formal and informal learning contexts were settings where positive effects of using mobile devices on language learning were found [7]. This implies mobile devices were functional to deliver language-learning materials and activities directly, such as for collaborative speaking and listening activities [14] as well as serving as learning supports.

Type of Test. Results indicated that positive treatment effects differed from zero only when language-learning achievement was assessed using researcher-made scales. Researcher-made scales were likely constructed to fit study goals and might measure specific areas that the researcher targeted and wanted to assess. Commercial standardized tests might assess broader areas of language achievement that students might not have learned from/on their mobile devices [60]. In contrast, researchers who create their own scales likely closely target the specific skills or vocabulary terms that were covered in their own m-learning applications. This could reflect the phenomenon of teaching to the test [61].

4.3. Significance of the Study

Similar to other reviews or meta-analysis studies that showed strong positive effects of mobile learning [4], this review also found medium sized positive effects of using mobile devices on language learning. Also in spite of the fact that effects varied between studies, in conditions similar to those in our studies, students receiving mobile-learning language instruction will almost always outscore others on average. In addition, the current review employed a comprehensive set of moderators to investigate the effects of various potential conditions on language-learning achievement which could lead to heterogeneity in the population. Only study source and type of test explained between studies differences. It is disconcerting that the effects of mobile learning were minimal when measured via standardized tests because, in many school settings, those are the tests of choice for assessment. School level, context of study, target language learning skill, type of test, and target language-learner group did not reach significance. This comprehensive moderator analysis contributed to understanding the various conditions for effective mobile-device use in language learning.

4.4. Limitations and Suggestions for Future Study

First, the results of our analysis for source of study showed that the mean effect size of journal articles ($d = 0.59$, $se = 0.10$) was significantly different from the mean effect size of dissertations

($d = 0.11$, $se = 0.22$). We suspect publication bias may have played a role in this result. Researchers have observed that publication bias arises from the tendency of journals to reject insignificant findings [62,63]. Therefore, using only journal articles as resources in prior meta-analyses may have led to skewed interpretations if their published studies were more likely to include significant results [64,65]. This was clearly the case for our studies. In future reviews, unpublished studies and reports should be included to ensure that conclusions that are more appropriate. When we applied the trim-and-fill technique to estimate the adjusted mean for the hypothetical full set of studies (including studies missing from the funnel plot), the estimated mean was still positive, but showed a smaller (and not significant) effect of using mobile devices for language learning ($d = 0.36$, $se = 0.03$).

Second, it might be useful to address more potential moderators in a meta-analysis study. For example, we would like to investigate the specifications of mobile devices such as screen size and operational system (i.e., OSX vs. Android). Sung et al. [7] found hardware specifications (e.g., handheld devices and laptops vs. mixed devices) influenced the heterogeneity of the effect sizes in their review. In addition, the effects of type of mobile application (e.g., commercial training vs. educational purposes) or additional target language skills such as language acquisition and language skill improvement can be addressed.

Third, this review investigated the effectiveness of mobile devices on the cognitive domain (i.e., language-learning achievement) across various moderators. In future studies, it may be fruitful to conduct research on the effects of using mobile devices in the affective domain, such as on learners' motivational status or attitudes toward language learning; and in the meta-cognitive domain, such as on learners' self-regulation and use of intellectual strategies [10].

Author Contributions: Joo and Lee conceived of the presented idea, collected the papers and wrote the initial draft. Cho verified the analytical methods, conducted analyses, wrote method and result and contributed to the interpretation of the results. Becker: provided advice about analyses, wrote parts of the text, edited text. All authors discusses the results and contributed to the final manuscript.

funding: This research received no external funding.

Conflicts of Interest: The authors declare no conflicts of interests.

References

1. Hwang, G.-J.; Tsai, C.-C. Research trends in mobile and ubiquitous learning: A review of publications in selected journals from 2001 to 2010. *Br. J. Educ. Technol.* **2011**, *42*, E65–E70. [CrossRef]
2. Sung, Y.-T.; Chang, K.-E.; Yang, J.-M. Review: How effective are mobile devices for language learning? A meta-analysis. *Educ. Res. Rev.* **2015**, *16*, 68–84. [CrossRef]
3. Wang, Y.-H. Integrating self-paced mobile learning into language instruction: Impact on reading comprehension and learner satisfaction. *Interact. Learn. Environ.* **2017**, *25*, 397–411. [CrossRef]
4. Wu, W.-H.; Wu, Y.-C.J.; Chen, C.-Y.; Kao, H.-Y.; Lin, C.-H.; Huang, S.-H. Review of trends from mobile learning studies: A meta-analysis. *Comput. Educ.* **2012**, *59*, 817–827. [CrossRef]
5. Joseph, S.; Uther, M. Mobile language learning with multimedia and multi-modal interfaces. In Proceedings of the 2006 Fourth IEEE International Workshop on Wireless, Mobile and Ubiquitous Technology in Education, Athens, Greece, 16–17 November 2006; IEEE: Piscataway, NJ, USA, 2006; p. 124.
6. Kim, P.H. Action research approach on mobile learning design for the underserved. *Educ. Technol. Res. Dev.* **2009**, *57*, 415–435. [CrossRef]
7. Sung, Y.-T.; Chang, K.-E.; Liu, T.-C. The effects of integrating mobile devices with teaching and learning on students' learning performance: A meta-analysis and research synthesis. *Comput. Educ.* **2016**, *94*, 252–275. [CrossRef]
8. Herrera Díaz, L.E.; Cruz Ramos, M.d.l.M.; Sandoval Sánchez, M.A. Using personal portable devices as learning tools in the english class. *How* **2014**, *21*, 74–93. [CrossRef]
9. Traxler, J.; Kukulska-Hulme, A. *Mobile Learning: A Handbook for Educators and Trainers*; Routledge: London, UK, 2005.

10. Viberg, O.; Grönlund, Å. Mobile assisted language learning: A literature review. In Proceedings of the 11th World Conference on Mobile and Contextual Learning, (mLearn 2012), Helsinki, Finland, 16–18 October 2012; Volume 955.

11. Hsu, C.-K.; Hwang, G.-J.; Chang, C.-K. A personalized recommendation-based mobile learning approach to improving the reading performance of EFL students. *Comput. Educ.* **2013**, *63*, 327–336. [CrossRef]

12. Klopfer, E.; Squire, K. Environmental detectives—The development of an augmented reality platform for environmental simulations. *Educ. Technol. Res. Dev.* **2008**, *56*, 203–228. [CrossRef]

13. Elfeky, A.I.M.; Masadeh, T.S.Y. The effect of mobile learning on students' achievement and conversational skills. *Int. J. High. Educ.* **2016**, *5*, 20–31. [CrossRef]

14. Kukulska-Hulme, A.; Shield, L. An overview of mobile assisted language learning: From content delivery to supported collaboration and interaction. *ReCall* **2008**, *20*, 271–289. [CrossRef]

15. Sandberg, J.; Maris, M.; de Geus, K. Mobile english learning: An evidence-based study with fifth graders. *Comput. Educ.* **2011**, *57*, 1334–1347. [CrossRef]

16. Yang, C.-C.; Hwang, G.-J.; Hung, C.-M.; Tseng, S.-S. An evaluation of the learning effectiveness of concept map-based science book reading via mobile devices. *J. Educ. Technol. Soc.* **2013**, *16*, 167–178.

17. Thornton, P.; Houser, C. Using mobile phones in English education in Japan. *J. Comput. Assist. Learn.* **2005**, *21*, 217–228. [CrossRef]

18. Hung, J.L.; Zhang, K. Examining mobile learning trends 2003–2008: A categorical meta-trend analysis using text mining techniques. *J. Comput. High. Educ.* **2012**, *24*, 1–17. [CrossRef]

19. Tingir, S.; Cavlazoglu, B.; Caliskan, O.; Koklu, O.; Intepe-Tingir, S. Effects of mobile devices on K-12 students' achievement: A meta-analysis. *J. Comput. Assist. Learn.* **2017**, *33*, 355–369. [CrossRef]

20. Khemaja, M.; Taamallah, A. Towards situation driven mobile tutoring system for learning languages and communication skills: Application to users with specific Needsneeds. *J. Educ. Technol. Soc.* **2016**, *19*, 113–128.

21. Lan, Y.-F.; Sie, Y.-S. Using RSS to support mobile learning based on media richness theory. *Comput. Educ.* **2010**, *55*, 723–732. [CrossRef]

22. Pisey, S.H.; Ramteke, P.L.; Burghate, B.R. Mobile learning transforming education & training. *Int. J. Adv. Res. Comput. Sci.* **2012**, *3*, 827–831.

23. Sharples, M. *Big Issues in Mobile Learning*; University of Nottingham: Nottingham, UK, 2006.

24. Purcell, K.; Heaps, A.; Buchanan, J.; Friedrich, L. How Teachers Are Using Technology at Home and in Their Classroom. Pew Research Center, 2013. Available online: http://pewinternet.org/Reports/2013/teachers-and-technology (accessed on 20 March 2013).

25. Huang, C.S.J.; Yang, S.J.H.; Chiang, T.H.C.; Su, A.Y.S. Effects of situated mobile learning approach on learning motivation and performance of EFL students. *J. Educ. Technol. Soc.* **2016**, *19*, 263–276.

26. Kukulska-Hulme, A. Will mobile learning change language learning? *ReCALL* **2009**, *21*, 157–165. [CrossRef]

27. Cavus, N.; Ibrahim, D. m-Learning: An experiment in using SMS to support learning new English language words. *Br. J. Educ. Technol.* **2009**, *40*, 78–91. [CrossRef]

28. Lu, M. Effectiveness of vocabulary learning via mobile phone. *J. Comput. Assist. Learn.* **2008**, *24*, 515–525. [CrossRef]

29. Chinnery, G.M. Going to the MALL: Mobile assisted language learning. *Lang. Learn. Technol.* **2006**, *10*, 9–16.

30. Chen, C.-M.; Chung, C.-J. Personalized mobile English vocabulary learning system based on item response theory and learning memory cycle. *Comput. Educ.* **2008**, *51*, 624–645. [CrossRef]

31. Rahimi, M.; Miri, S.S. The impact of mobile dictionary use on language learning. *Procedia Soc. Behav. Sci.* **2014**, *98*, 1469–1474. [CrossRef]

32. Ho, S.-C.; Hsieh, S.-W.; Sun, P.-C.; Chen, C.-M. To activate English learning: Listen and speak in real life context with an AR featured u-learning system. *Educ. Technol. Soc.* **2017**, *20*, 176–187.

33. Kenning, M.M. *ICT and Language Learning: From Print to the Mobile Phone*; Palgrave Macmillan: Basingstoke, UK; New York, NY, USA, 2007.

34. Saffran, J.R.; Senghas, A.; Trueswell, J.C. The acquisition of language by children. *Proc. Natl. Acad. Sci. USA* **2001**, *98*, 12874–12875. [CrossRef] [PubMed]

35. Brown, L. Using Mobile Learning to Teach Reading to Ninth-Grade Students. Ph.D. Dissertation, Capella University, Minneapolis, MN, USA, November 2008.

36. Fishburn, T.A. Mobile Device Reading Interventions in the Kindergarten Classroom. Ph.D. Dissertation, Wilmington University (Delaware), Ann Arbor, MI, USA, November 2008.

37. Zhang, H.; Song, W.; Burston, J. Reexamining the effectiveness of vocabulary learning via mobile phones. *Turk. Online J. Educ. Technol. TOJET* **2011**, *10*, 203–214.
38. Murat, S.; Gölge, S.; Kürşat, Ç. Mobile assisted language learning: English pronunciation at learners' fingertips. *Eurasian J. Educ. Res.* **2009**, *34*, 97–114.
39. Ahmad Zamzuri Mohamad, A.; Kogilathah, S.; Tan Wee, H. Effects of verbal components in 3D talking-head on pronunciation learning among non-native speakers. *J. Educ. Technol. Soc.* **2015**, *18*, 313–322.
40. Basoglu, E.B.; Akdemir, O. A comparison of undergraduate students' English vocabulary learning: Using mobile phones and flash cards. *Turk. Online J. Educ. Technol. TOJET* **2010**, *9*, 1–7.
41. Billings, E.; Mathison, C. I get to use an iPod in school? Using technology-based advance organizers to support the academic success of English learners. *J. Sci. Educ. Technol.* **2012**, *21*, 494–503. [CrossRef]
42. Kétyi, A. Practical evaluation of a mobile language learning tool in higher education. In Proceedings of the 2015 EUROCALL Conference, Padova, Italy, 26–29 August 2015.
43. Khrisat, A.A.; Mahmoud, S.S. Integrating mobile phones into the EFL foundation year classroom in King Abdulaziz University/KSA: Effects on achievement in general English and students' attitudes. *Eng. Lang. Teach.* **2013**, *6*, 162–174. [CrossRef]
44. Kondo, M.; Ishikawa, Y.; Smith, C.; Sakamoto, K.; Shimomura, H.; Wada, N. Mobile assisted language learning in university EFL courses in Japan: Developing attitudes and skills for self-regulated learning. *ReCALL* **2012**, *24*, 169–187. [CrossRef]
45. Mellati, M.; Khademi, M. The impacts of distance interactivity on learners' achievements in online mobile language learning: Social software and participatory learning. *Int. J. Web Based Learn. Teach. Technol.* **2015**, *10*, 19–35. [CrossRef]
46. Murat, S.; Gölge, S.; Kürşat, Ç. Mobile language learning: Contribution of multimedia messages via mobile phones in consolidating vocabulary. *Asia Pac. Educ. Res. Salle Univ. Manila* **2012**, *21*, 181–190.
47. Walters, J.L. English Language Learners' Reading Self-Efficacy and Achievement Using 1:1 Mobile Learning Devices. Ph.D. Dissertation, University of California, San Diego, CA, USA, 2012.
48. Wu, T.T.; Huang, Y.M. Mobile game-based english vocabulary practice system based on portfolio analysis. *J. Educ. Technol. Soc.* **2017**, *20*, 265–277.
49. Comas-Quinn, A.; Mardomingo, R.; Valentine, C. Mobile blogs in language learning: Making the most of informal and situated learning opportunities. *ReCALL* **2009**, *21*, 96–112. [CrossRef]
50. Marsick, V.J.; Watkins, K.E. Informal and incidental learning. *New Dir. Adult Contin. Educ.* **2001**, *89*, 25–34. [CrossRef]
51. Sidik, K.; Jonkman, J.N. Robust variance estimation for random effects meta-analysis. *Comput. Stat. Data Anal.* **2006**, *50*, 3681–3701. [CrossRef]
52. Lipsey, M.W.; Wilson, D.B. *Practical Meta-Analysis*; Sage Publications: Thousand Oaks, CA, USA, 2001.
53. Rothstein, H.R. Publication bias as a threat to the validity of meta-analytic results. *J. Exp. Criminol.* **2008**, *4*, 61–68. [CrossRef]
54. Rothstein, H.R.; Sutton, A.J.; Borenstein, M. Publication bias: Recognizing the problem, understanding its origins and scope, and preventing harm. In *Publication Bias in Meta-Analysis: Prevention, Assessment & Adjustments*; Wiley: Hoboken, NJ, USA, 2005.
55. Borenstein, M.; Hedges, L.V.; Higgins, J.P.T.; Rothstein, H.R. A basic introduction to fixed-effect and random-effects models for meta-analysis. *Res. Synth. Methods* **2010**, *1*, 97–111. [CrossRef] [PubMed]
56. Effer, M.; Davey Smith, G.; Schneider, M.; Minder, C. Bias in meta-analysis detected by a simple, graphical test. *BMJ Br. Med. J.* **1997**, *315*, 629. [CrossRef]
57. Stockwell, G. Using mobile phones for vocabulary activities: Examining the effect of the platform. *Lang. Learn. Technol.* **2010**, *14*, 95–110.
58. De Jong, T.; Specht, M.; Koper, R. A study of contextualised mobile information delivery for language learning. *Educ. Technol. Soc.* **2010**, *13*, 110–125.
59. Mahdi, H.S. Effectiveness of mobile devices on vocabulary learning: A meta-analysis. *J. Educ. Comput. Res.* **2018**, *56*, 134–154. [CrossRef]
60. Braus, J.A.; Wood, D.S. *Environmental Education in the Schools: Creating a Program that Works!* NAAEE: Washington, DC, USA, 1994.
61. Phakiti, A. *Experimental Research Methods in Language Learning*; Bloomsbury Academic: New York, NY, USA, 2015.

62. Sterne, J.A.; Gavaghan, D.; Egger, M. Publication and related bias in meta-analysis: Power of statistical tests and prevalence in the literature. *J. Clin. Epidemiol.* **2000**, *53*, 1119–1129. [CrossRef]

63. Thornton, A.; Lee, P. Original articles: Publication bias in meta-analysis. its causes and consequences. *J. Clin. Epidemiol.* **2000**, *53*, 207–216. [CrossRef]

64. Adesope, O.O.; Lavin, T.; Thompson, T.; Ungerleider, C. A systematic review and meta-analysis of the cognitive correlates of bilingualism. *Rev. Educ. Res.* **2010**, *80*, 207–245. [CrossRef]

65. Song, F.; Hooper, L.; Loke, Y.K. Publication bias: What is it? How do we measure it? How do we avoid it? *Open Access J. Clin. Trials* **2013**, *2013*, 71–81. [CrossRef]

Article

Attitude towards Mobile Learning in English Language Education

Cemil Yurdagül [1],* and Saba Öz [2],*

[1]   Vocational School of Justice, Ankara University, 06560 Cebeci/Ankara, Turkey
[2]   Department of Computer Education and Instructional Technology, Middle East Technical University,
     06800 Çankaya/Ankara, Turkey
*   Correspondence: cyurdagul@ankara.edu.tr (C.Y.); saba@metu.edu.tr (S.O.); Tel.: +90-312-595-52-51 (C.Y.)

Received: 22 April 2018; Accepted: 7 July 2018; Published: 10 September 2018

Abstract: Mobile devices, especially smart phones, are the most frequently used technological devices for daily routines. Mobile devices can be used for various purposes to meet different needs. Since education is a core requirement for human beings, smart phones are being integrated into education. However, it remains to be seen whether they have an impact on learning or not. Consequently, integration of these technologies, or "mobile learning", has become a popular research study in the field of instructional technology. It is important to investigate the impact of smart phones in language education since students today use them frequently. This attitudinal study aims to investigate the attitude of students in higher education towards smart phone use in the context of foreign language learning. In particular, it gathers information about how smart phones are used for language learning. Participants of the study were 294 prep school students from a well-known university in Turkey. Descriptive study was selected as a research method and mixed-method was the research design for the study. The findings of the study showed that participants care about instant and easy access to information in language learning. In addition to drawing attention to the ease of information access, participants provided suggestions about future applications of smartphones in language learning.

Keywords: mobile learning; English language teaching; attitude; language learning; smartphone; technology integration

1. Introduction

Mobile devices, especially smartphones, are the most frequently used technological devices in daily routines. They have been used for more than three decades since their invention. The first generation of mobile devices are mobile phones, invented in 1990s, through which people could only make a call and send short messages (SMS). As technology improved so fast, mobile phones took smaller and more intelligent forms thus started to be named smartphones. Providing so many advantages, smartphones replaced desktop computers and even notebooks [1,2] (p. 1). They did so because these mobile and functional devices are " ... handheld telecommunication devices that combine miniaturized hardware of a personal computer and a mobile phone with relatively large touch screen" [3] (p. 427).

As a result of rapid development of mobile technologies and their integration into education, the term "mobile learning" emerged. Kukulska-Hulme and Traxler [4] conceptualize mobile learning as "it is certainly concerned with learner mobility, in the sense that learners should be able to engage in educational activities without the constraint of having to do so in a tightly delimited physical location" (p. 1). In their mobile learning concept, it is clear that mobile learning is concerned with learners and learning mobility rather than mobility of technological devices. Within this scope, mobile learning covers the mobility of learners, mobility of learning, mobility of educators or instructors and mobility of technological devices [5]. It is noteworthy that mobile learning is not only learning that is based heavily on the use of mobile devices, but also learning that is mediated across contexts using portable technologies [5,6].

Rapid development of mobile technology has sped up the popularity and proliferation of mobile handheld devices. They provide various functions such as voiced navigation for vehicles, communication and network facilities through social media applications (Facebook, Twitter, Instagram, WhatsApp etc.), 3G/4G visual communication, web browsing, online banking, photo and video shooting, sharing applications, and games. At the same time, smartphones are getting more user-friendly and increasing their functionality level. As their functionality continuously expands, they remain efficient and easy to use [7]. That is, users spend less time managing resource access and more time evaluating the value of those resources [8]. Inevitably, they are widely used and becoming a basic need for communicative and technological interactions.

As well as providing mobility, mobile devices offer numerous opportunities. Time of knowledge access, and time and place independency (known as ubiquitous computing) for information search are just two examples. Another term in the related literature for just-in-time knowledge gain is Just-In-Time Learning (JITL) which refers to "brief educational experiences targeted to a specific need" [9]. Furthermore, mobile devices enable individuals to access knowledge practically and on the spot [10]. They also allow access to knowledge everywhere during transportation, during outdoor activities etc. [11]. People can reach information by using mobile devices even while sitting in a restaurant or waiting for a bus without the restrictions of desktop computer technology [8]. Considering all these remarkable advantages of mobile devices, it is possible to predict the extent to which smartphones will be used for educational purposes. For the time being, mobile devices are mostly used for entertainment, information sharing, and connecting to social network sites [12] in leisure times, despite their potential educational advantages and benefits as follows: adaptation of learning to students' learning styles and preferences; interactive learning; multimedia capabilities; ubiquitous Internet connectivity; increased understanding of learning materials; increase in students' motivation; cost-effectiveness; enhanced communication between teachers and students; easy access; student-friendliness; and effective feedback [13–17] (p. 1). Dashtestani states that these advantages and benefits of mobile learning and mobile technologies have already encouraged several educational institutions and organizations to think of mobile technologies as the new learning medium of the current era for both students and instructors and shift their focus from e-learning to mobile learning when designing educational settings. Furthermore, Kinash et al. [18] argue that young generations in particular are already familiar with mobile technologies. Therefore, students should be encouraged to use smartphones to reach and practice learning materials.

Mobile technologies have many advantages for foreign language learning. Thanks to continuous connection to the Internet, students can reach any kind of information everywhere and anytime with respect to language learning. By considering the potential of mobile technologies for language learning, Traxler [19] states that "it is possible to make language learning more authentic, efficient, relevant, and effective by recognizing and responding to universal mobile technologies" (p. 2). Therefore, it is important to provide students with authentic and contemporary language learning environments by benefiting from advantages of mobile technologies. Furthermore, Ogato and Yano [20] claim that mobile technologies are beneficial for language learning since they believe language learning is much more related to context and situations in which learning occurs.

It seems that designers of mobile educational applications are increasingly interested in foreign language learning since students often need to access instant linguistic information, e.g., they look up the meaning of words or conjugation/collocations. However, it is important to conduct some attitudinal and descriptive studies before developing mobile learning applications in a pre-determined subject area to save time and cost. In this regard, learners' perceptions of use of mobile devices for educational purposes should be inspected as it may shed light on their motives for using mobile technologies. Moreover, attitudes towards any kind of educational technology could be used to measure to what extent users of such technology (learners and instructors) have ambitions to use the specific technology [5,21]. Ally [2] remarks that the main reason behind the unsuccessful or ineffective implementation of mobile technologies for educational purposes is the attitude of people toward the use of such technologies in education. Therefore, the main purpose of this descriptive study is to inspect the attitude of university-level English language learners towards the use of mobile devices. Indeed, it intends to obtain pre-knowledge about their mobile technology experience in general and in language learning, and elicit their opinions and suggestions, which then will guide further mobile English language learning applications and the related literature. To this end, the study seeks to answers to the following research questions:

RQ1. What is the attitude of prep-school students towards mobile learning?

RQ1a. Is there a significant difference among the students' attitudes towards mobile learning in terms of gender?

RQ1b. Is there a significant difference among the students' attitudes towards mobile learning in terms of faculty?

RQ2. For what purpose do prep-school students use mobile technologies?

RQ3. To what extent do prep-school students use mobile technologies for language learning?

RQ4. Which applications or websites are used by prep-school students in terms of language learning?

RQ5. What are the opinions of prep-school students about the design of mobile learning environments for language learning?

2. Methodology

This descriptive study focuses on higher education students' attitude towards mobile learning in English language learning. Since the aim of this study is best fit, embedded type mixed-method research design was applied. Embedded design provides collecting quantitative and qualitative data simultaneously or sequentially just as in parallel or sequential mixed-method design; however, one form of data (qualitative or quantitative) plays a supportive role to other form of data [22]. This is the key point of embedded design, in which both qualitative and quantitative forms of data are collected simultaneously (or sequentially) and results are formed together to explain the research problem. The reason for collecting a second form of data is to enhance or augment findings shown in the first form of data, which can be both qualitative or quantitative, although the more commonly used type in literature is adding qualitative data into quantitative design [22]. For this study, a qualitative form of data was used for augmenting or supporting quantitative form. Quantitative data were obtained from a questionnaire called the mobile learning attitude scale (MLAS) [23] and qualitative data were obtained from taking written responses of students by providing a demographic information form.

2.1. Sample, Sampling Technique and Study Instrument

The subjects of the study are 294 prep-school students from the Middle East Technical University (METU), one of the well-known universities in Turkey. Prep-school in higher education means school of foreign language education served for prep-year university students. Among them, 157 are female and 137 are male whose ages are between 18 and 30 (for distribution of ages see Figure 1 below). A convenience sampling approach was used as a sampling technique. There was no criterion for selecting subjects except for being in the same level (pre-intermediate) of English in order to keep consistency among subjects and language level effect minimum. The instruments used in the study are mobile learning attitude scale (MLAS) [23] and demographical information form in which some demographics and open-ended items are involved in order to gather some extra information for the qualitative part of the study. Mobile learning attitude scale [23] consists of 4 sub-factors as advantages of m-learning, constraints of m-learning, usefulness of m-learning, and freedom in m-learning by involving 21 items with a 5-point Likert-type scale. For naming of factors, sub-items combined in the same factor were carefully examined and proposed factor names finalized after taking opinions of two different field experts [23]. For the reliability issue of the MLAS, it was shown that MLAS is adequate for differentiating participants with positive attitudes from those possessing negative ones [23]. For the validity of the MLAS, it was shown that scale has a high internal consistency (Cronbach α = 0.88) [23]. A demographical information form was developed by the researchers and includes gender, age, department, frequency of Internet use, and mobile technology use. Moreover, some open-ended items were added in order to support quantitative data by asking the aim of mobile technology use with respect to language learning, benefits of using mobile learning environments, types of mobile applications used for language learning, and design suggestions for a mobile application in foreign language learning.

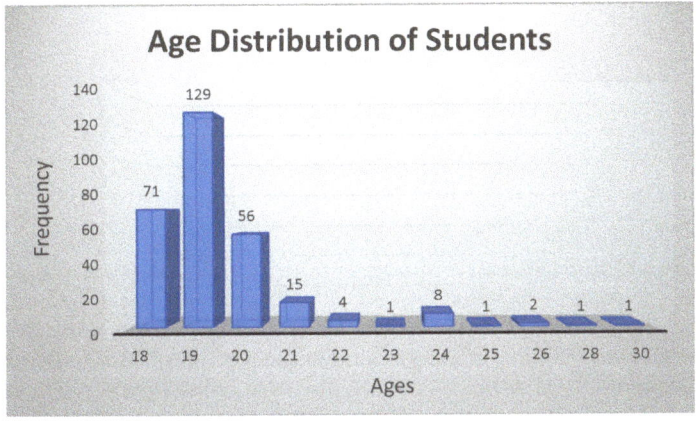

Figure 1. Age distribution of students.

2.2. Measurement and Analysis

To answer research questions that form the basis of the study, an independent sample t-test and one-way ANOVA statistical techniques were applied by using the statistical analysis program SPSS. For demographical information (age, gender, faculty, and department), descriptive analysis techniques of SPSS were applied. For qualitative data collected from open-ended questions in the demographical information form, document analysis was conducted. Document analysis was used for extraction of participants' statements related to research questions guiding the study. Therefore, no any special coding technique was applied. Instead, statements provided by the participants were carefully selected by relevance and involved in corresponding sections of results to support descriptive findings.

3. Results

3.1. Demographical Information

Among the students participating in the study (294 prep-school students), 157 were female and 137 were male. Their ages ranged between 18 and 30 with an average of 19 (Figure 1).

Among participants, 15 (5%) students were registered to the Faculty of Architecture, 69 (24%) were registered to the Faculty of Arts and Sciences, 38 (13%) were registered to the Faculty of Economic and Administrative Sciences, 69 (24%) were registered to the Faculty of Education and 99 (34%) were registered to the Faculty of Engineering (see Figure 2 below).

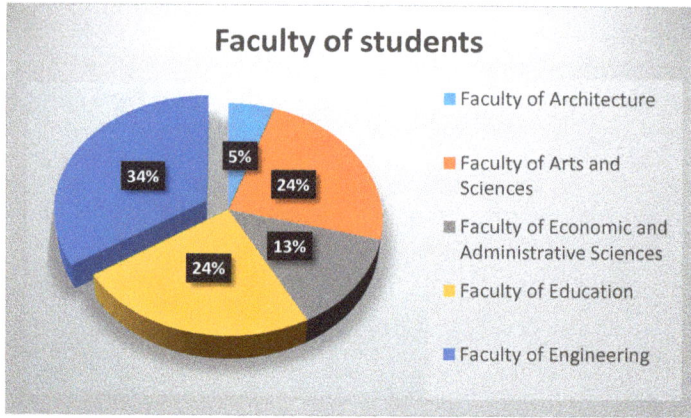

Figure 2. Faculty distribution of students.

3.2. Results of Qualitative Data Analysis

Participants provided an item for frequency of Internet use in order to gain an idea about how many hours per day students spend on Internet use. The reason for this was to see their Internet usage, which may guide future design plans for mobile language learning application by deciding whether to design online or offline learning environments. Frequency of their daily Internet use is grouped into 5 categories as: (1) below 1 h per day; (2) between 1 and 2 h per day; (3) between 3 and 4 h per day; (4) between 4 and 5 h per day; and (5) above 5 h per day. These are shown below in Figure 3. Among participants, 10 use the Internet less than 1 h per day (4%), 53 use the Internet between 1 and 2 h per day (18%), 100 use the Internet between 3 and 4 h per day (34%), 62 use the Internet between 4 and 5 h per day, and 68 use the Internet more than 5 h per day (23%).

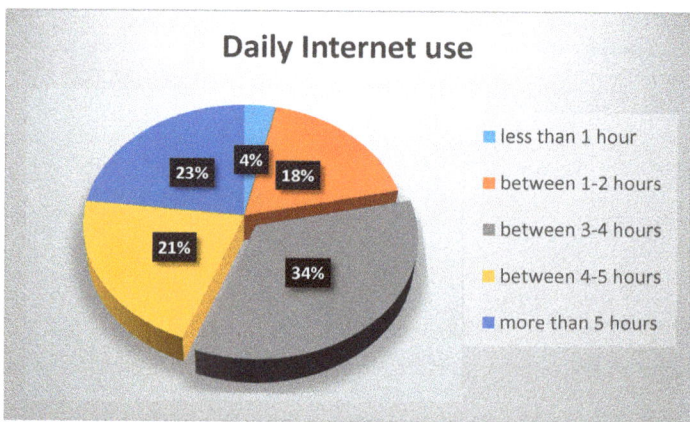

Figure 3. Daily Internet use of students.

Participants were also asked what percent of their total Internet use belongs to their mobile devices in order to inspect the frequency of Internet use by their mobile devices. It was found that 16 met less than 10% of their total Internet use with their mobile devices, 22 met more than 10% and less than 30% of their total Internet use with their mobile devices, 42 met more than 30% and less than

50% of their total Internet use with their mobile devices, 58 met more than 50% and less than 70% of their total Internet use with their mobile devices, 61 met more than 70% and less than 90% of their total Internet use with their mobile devices and 95 of them met more than 90% of their total Internet use with their mobile devices (see Figure 4). This shows that majority of students prefer to use mobile devices for Internet.

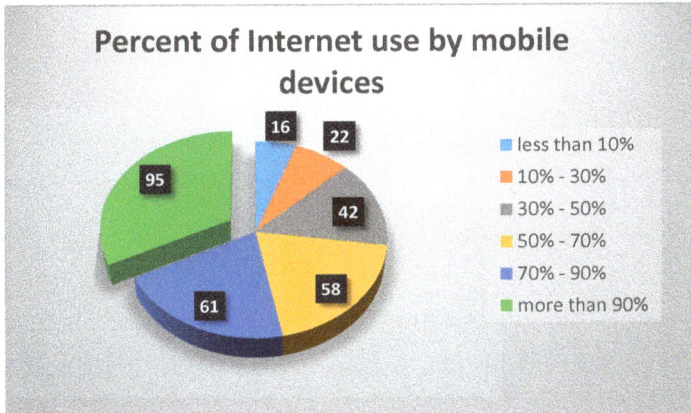

Figure 4. Students' percent of Internet use by mobile devices.

Students were also asked about the purpose of using mobile devices, which is grouped into 4 categories: communication; social media; educational purpose; and other. 257 participants used mobile devices as a communication tool, 251 used mobile devices for social media, and 187 used mobile devices for an educational purpose. This can be interpreted as students preferring to use mobile devices for mostly communicative and social media purposes. Some participants provided other purposes for which they use mobile devices, such as: gaming; banking; online shopping; watching TV or films; listening to music; entertainment; taking photos; and PDF viewing. Students were not only asked about the general purpose of using mobile devices but also they were asked about the aim of using mobile devices in language learning. Students' answers were transcribed into 382 codes and 16 purposes of mobile device use in language learning (see Figure 5). These purposes are given with their corresponding percentages as follows: use of dictionary (55%); listening to language learning materials (8%); topic repetition (10%); listening to music (2%); watching language learning videos (2%); watching films (4%); writing practice (1%); practicing collocation (1%); undertaking research (1%); practicing vocabulary (8%); reading practice (1%); translation (4%); pronunciation (1%); using language learning applications (1%); and chatting with foreign friends (1%). It is necessary to explain two categories in Figure 4 that may cause confusion and seem similar but indeed are not. These are watching films and watching videos. "Watching films" means watching any kind of film which is not directly related to language learning. However, "watching videos" means watching videos for supporting language learning. As seen from the results, the majority of students use mobile devices in language learning for a dictionary. Then topic repetition and listening materials follows.

The subjects were also asked to state their opinions about the advantages of mobile devices, and results are shown below (Figure 6).

As seen from Figure 5, the majority of participants think that mobile devices are advantageous for providing rapid access (44%) and easy access (26%) and supportive for leaning (10%) follows this. Two categories in Figure 5 may seem similar but indeed are not. These are "supportive for learning" and "beneficial for English learning". The reason behind the separation of these categories is that mobile devices can be used for learning everything, whether related to curriculum or not.

Therefore, "supportive for learning" refers to learning in general and "beneficial for English learning" specifically refers to the advantage of mobile devices for language learning. Participants also stated some opinions about the advantage of mobile devices. Some of statements provided by them are given below:

"Bilgilere hızlıca ulaşıyorum, Tenefüslerde, otobüslerde, otobüs beklerken filan kulanıyorum ve faydalı buluyorum".

"I can access information quickly during break time of my courses, on buses, while waiting for a bus, and I think it is beneficial" (participant 34).

"Kelimelerin anlamlarını daha hızlı öğrenmek için ve bazı grammer konularını tekrar için daha hızlı ulaşabliyorum".

"I can access information quickly in order to learn meanings of words more quickly and to repeat some grammar issues" (participant 78).

"Herşey daha hızlı ve yanımızda istediğimiz an istediğimiz şeye ulaşabiliyoruz".

"Everything is quicker and near us, so we can reach whatever we want whenever we want" (participant 57).

"Hemen elimizin altında sözlük bulunuyor öğretmen olmadığı zaman bir konuyu sorabiliyoruz".

"With these mobile devices we have a dictionary in our hands so we can reach everything we want to ask when our instructor is not available" (participants 189).

The above statements give a clue about the way mobile devices are used by students. As understood by the statements provided by the students, the main advantage of mobile devices is the quick and easy access to information everywhere. With respect to language learning, mobile devices provide easy ways to look for meanings of words (online dictionaries) and grammar practice.

Participants were asked which websites and mobile applications they use frequently for the purpose of language learning (Table 1). Among their responses, prominent ones are Tureng (an online dictionary) (46%), Quizlet (online practical language learning materials) (6%), TED (expert videos for various topics) (7%), Sesli Sözlük (an online dictionary) (5%) and Google Translate (5%).

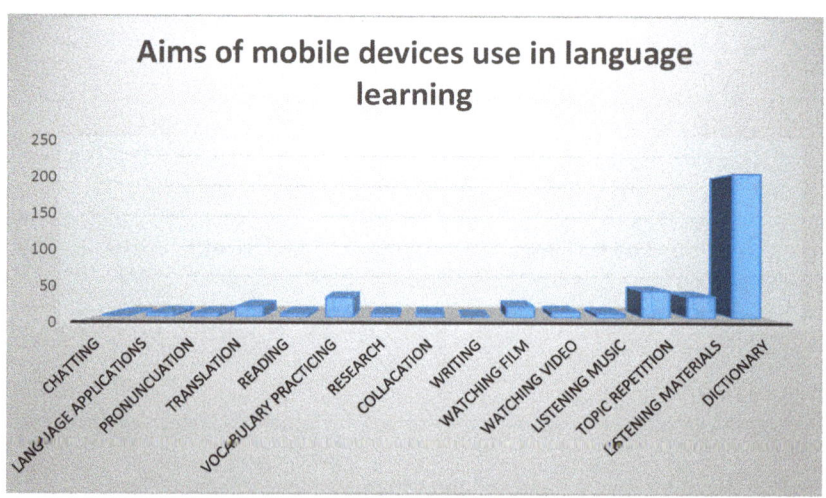

Figure 5. Students' aims of mobile devices use in language learning.

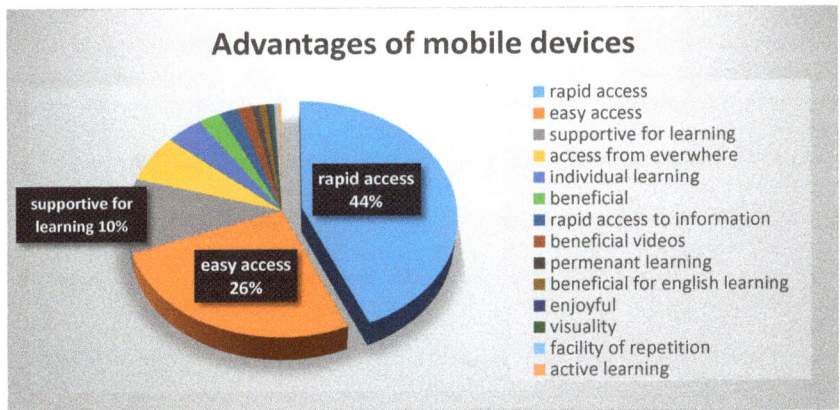

Figure 6. Students' opinions about advantages of mobile devices.

Table 1. Websites and mobile applications used by students for language learning.

Websites & Mobile Application	Frequency
Tureng	121
TED	18
Quizlet	17
Sesli Sözlük	14
Google Translate	13
Oxford Dictionary	11
British Council	10
Memrise	9
Duolingo	9
Voscreen	6
Cambridge Dictionary	6
Longman Active Study Dictionary	4
Macmillan	4
LinguaLeo	3
Yandex	3
BBC	3
British Council Podcast	1
News in Levels	1
Dyned	1
Quara	1
Coursera	1
Ozdic	1
WhatsApp	1
EDx	1
Meriam Webster	1
Dictionary	2
Zargan Dictionary	1

When Table 1 is examined overall, it is seen that majority of websites or applications provided by students are based on dictionary use as Tureng, Sesli Sözlük, Oxford Dictionary, Cambridge Dictionary, Longman Active Dictionary, Macmillan, Ozdic, Meriam Webster, and Zargan. Students also provided some translation websites (i.e., Google Translate) and some language practice or online language education websites/applications (i.e., Memrise, Quizlet, Duolingo, LinguaLeo, Dyned). Furthermore, some short video-providing websites/applications for language learning practice were also preferred by students (i.e., TED, Voscreen, BBC, British Council Podcast). Students also preferred to practice their English by using some interactive learning environments such as Quara, through which users ask questions and offer answers among themselves. Thinking more comprehensively, some students cited the use of online course enrollment by using well-known websites as Coursera and EDx. Briefly, if websites/applications preferred by students for language learning are grouped into categories, 5 main categories can be made: (1) dictionary/translation; (2) language practicing; (3) video-based language learning; (4) interactive language learning; and (5) online courses.

Opinions of students regarding the design of mobile learning environments in terms of language learning were taken as well (Table 2). They stated 25 design suggestions for mobile applications. Prominent design suggestions are designing a mobile application for vocabulary practicing (24%), designing a more effective and useful dictionary (14%), designing a mobile application for practicing collocations (9%) and designing a mobile application for listening practice (9%).

Table 2. Opinions of students about the design of mobile learning environment.

Design Suggestions	Frequency
Vocabulary practicing	23
More effective and useful dictionary	14
Collocation practicing	9
Listening practice	9
Entertainment	9
Grammar	6
Speaking practice	3
Conversation	3
Reading Practice	3
Using vocabularies in sentences	3
Proficiency exam practice	2
Prioritizing visual memory	2
e.g., Duolingo	1
e.g., Voscreen	1
Consistent with used workbooks	1
Question and answer application such as quiz shows	1
Game-based and pronunciation-based	1
Chatting and talking with foreign friends	1
User-friendly and visually rich	1
Topic-related film and series video parts	1
Optimum level for all users	1
Translation	1
Translation of phrasal verbs	1

Table 2 offers clues about students' future preferences of mobile device use for language learning. When Table 2 is examined overall, it can be seen that students give importance to vocabulary practice and dictionary use. However, they emphasized that dictionaries should be more effective and useful. They also want to practice language sections such as reading, listening and speaking. Furthermore, they suggested that developers think about exam practice when they develop an application for language learning. Collocations and grammar use are also important topic for language learning and a respectable amount of suggestions are in this direction for developing future language learning mobile applications. Some suggestions are related to designing interactive applications such as question and answer, chatting and talking with foreign friends, game-based and entertaining learning environments. Briefly, students demand more beneficial, user-friendly and at the same time entertaining mobile learning environments for English language practice instead of book-based and non-interactive ones.

Some statements provided by students with respect to suggestions for future design of mobile learning environments regarding foreign language learning are given below:

"Kelimeleri cümle içinde kullanan bir uygulama çünkü bazı kelimelerin collocationları var"

"An application that uses vocabularies in sentences since some words have their collocations." (participant 179)

"Online yarışma şeklinde bu şekilde daha kolay bağımlılık yapıyor ve öğrenmek için değil eğlenmek için gelindiğinde daha etkili oluyor"

"I like online competitions since they make us more dependent on engaging in that way and when we use them for entertainment purposes rather than learn something, it is more effective." (participant 264)

"Çok amaçlı bir sözlük tasarlardım.Her sözcük için kurulu cümlelerin olduğu, hem türkçesinin hem ingilizcesinin ve bütün kullanımlarının oldugu bir uygulama tasarladım."

"I may design a multi-purpose dictionary application in which there are example sentences for each word, Turkish and English equivalents of each word, and their usage as well." (participant 91)

The above statements provided by students with respect to design suggestions for future mobile foreign language learning environments shows that students put more emphasis on practicing some specific language sections such as collocations and vocabulary use in sentences. Furthermore, it is possible to say in light of given suggestions that students prefer to learn/practice English by entertainment such as competition rather than focusing on learning something.

3.3. Results of Quantitative Data Analysis

Quantitative data obtained from the mobile learning attitude scale were used to answer the first research question, which tries to discover whether there is a significant difference among the students' attitudes towards mobile learning in terms of their gender and faculty. To clarify this, an independent t-test and one-way ANOVA techniques were applied.

The independent t-test was applied in order to clarify whether there are significant differences among the students' attitudes towards mobile learning in terms of gender (Table 3), and the result showed that there is not a significant difference between male students' ($M = 2.83$, $SD = 0.63$) attitude towards mobile learning and female students' ($M = 2.72$, $SD = 0.56$) attitude towards mobile learning $t(292) = -1.52$, $p = 0.13$.

One-way analysis of variance was conducted in order to examine whether there is a significant difference among students regarding attitude towards mobile learning in terms of faculties. The dependent variable was the attitude towards mobile learning score. The independent variable was the faculties of students, which included five levels (Table 4) as follows: faculty of architecture ($M = 2.77$, $SD = 0.46$); faculty of arts and sciences ($M = 2.60$, $SD = 0.61$); faculty of economics and administrative sciences ($M = 2.71$, $SD = 0.63$); faculty of education ($M = 2.89$, $SD = 0.52$); and faculty of engineering ($M = 2.82$, $SD = 0.61$). The results of ANOVA showed that there is a significant difference among students' attitude towards mobile learning in terms of faculties, $F(4285) = 2.49$, $p < 0.05$, $\eta^2 = 0.03$. The strength of relationship between the faculty groups and the attitude score of students toward mobile learning as assessed by η^2, was low, with the faculty groups accounting for 3% of the variance of the dependent variable (Table 5). Post-hoc comparisons indicated that the mean score for the faculty of education group ($M = 2.89$, $SD = 0.52$) was significantly different from the faculty of arts and sciences ($M = 2.71$, $SD = 0.63$).

Table 3. *t*-test result of comparing males and females on attitude towards mobile learning.

Gender	*n*	Mean	SD	t-cal	t-crit	df	p
Female	157	2.72	0.56	−1.52	1.96	292	0.13
Male	137	2.83	0.63				

Table 4. Faculty distribution among students.

Faculty Groups	Mean	SD	n
Faculty of Architecture	2.77	0.46	15
Faculty of Arts and Sciences	2.60	0.61	69
Faculty of Economics and Administrative Sciences	2.71	0.63	38
Faculty of Education	2.89	0.52	69
Faculty of Engineering	2.82	0.61	99

Table 5. One-way ANOVA results comparing faculties of students on attitude towards mobile learning.

Source	SS	df	MS	F	η^2
Faculty group	3.44	4	0.86	2.49 *	0.03
Error	98.34	285	0.35		
Total	101.78	289			

* $p < 0.05$.

4. Discussion and Conclusions

This study aims to explore attitudes of prep-school students towards mobile learning in order to gain deep insight about their point of view before designing and developing such language learning mobile applications. Participants were given a demographical information form and an attitude towards mobile learning scale. By analyzing quantitative and qualitative data obtained from these instruments, 5 research questions that form the basis of the study were asked. The results of study are discussed below in line with these questions:

RQ1a. Comparing males and females in terms of attitude towards mobile learning

Analysis result showed that there is no significant difference between male and female students' attitudes towards mobile learning. Similarly, some scholars have not found significant differences among students' attitudes toward the use of mobile learning in terms of their gender [5,24–26]. Furthermore, Uzunboylu, Cavus and Ercag [27] did not find significant difference between male students and female students in terms of the usefulness of mobile learning system [28] scores. Moreover, Rees and Noyes [29] did not find any difference between female and male mobile phone use. On the other hand, some researchers claim the opposite by indicating significant differences among the students' attitudes toward the use of mobile learning in terms of their gender, where female students were more positive towards the use of mobile phones compared to their male peers [30,31]. In terms of mobile phone use, Rees and Noyes found an interesting result that suggested males use voice calling more than females, while females use SMS more than males [29]. This may give a clue about males being prone to oral communication rather than written communication. Concerning gender, Skog [32] found that preferences of mobile phone differs as males focused on technical functions while females give importance to social aspects [33] (p. 283). Furthermore, in their descriptive study about students' mobile learning practices in higher education, Chen and Denoyelles [34] found that in terms of gender difference, males tended to use mobile devices for academic purposes more than females.

RQ1b. Comparing Faculties in terms of attitude towards mobile learning

Results showed that there is a significant difference among students' attitude towards mobile learning in terms of their faculty. In particular, it was observed that attitude score of students whose majors are from the faculty of education is greater than students whose majors are from the faculty of arts and sciences. Although it is hard to surmise certainly about this issue, it can be claimed that students from faculty of education are more prone to use of language learning-themed mobile applications than students from the faculty of arts and sciences. On the other hand, Al-Emran, Elsherif, and Shaalan [5] found that there are no significant differences among students' attitude toward mobile learning in terms of their academic majors. In terms of academic year, Chen and Denoyelles [34] found that freshmen and sophomores tended to use mobile devices in their courses more often than juniors and seniors. These results coincide with the result of this study in some way since the students participating in the current study are in the first year of their study at university.

RQ2. Purpose of using mobile technologies

Results showed that mobile technologies are mostly used for communication and social media purposes. In addition to these, mobile technologies are also used incontrovertibly by participants for an educational purpose. Apart from these, results of the study also showed that mobile technologies are used for different purposes such as gaming, banking, online shopping, watching TV or films, listening to music, entertainment, taking photos, and PDF viewing. In addition to these forms of mobile technology use, participants also stressed the quick access to the any kind of information through these kinds of technologies everywhere and at any time. This finding is parallel with Al-Fahad's [35] study which states that "mobile technologies are more flexible and enable students greater freedom of learning any place, any time" (p. 114).

RQ3. Purpose of using mobile technologies regarding language learning

In terms of language learning, it was found that mobile technologies are used by participants for different purposes in terms of language learning and language practicing. These purposes can be listed as follows: use of dictionary; listening language learning materials; making topic repetition; listening to music; watching language learning videos; watching films; writing practice; practicing collocation; making research; practicing vocabulary; reading practice; translation; pronunciation; using language learning applications; and chatting with foreign friends. In addition, participants stated that language learning is more entertaining when sharing information through chatting and competing. This finding coincides with the study of Chen and Denoyelles [34] which states that students perceived mobile technologies as powerful learning aids in terms of easy knowledge sharing and retrieval.

RQ4. Applications and websites used for language learning

Results showed that students mostly used Tureng, Quizlet, TED, Sesli Sözlük (an online dictionary website designed in Turkey) and Google Translate. In addition to them, Oxford Dictionary, British Council, Memrise and Cambridge Dictionary websites were used most by prep-school students. These results can be interpreted as students using their mobile devices to look up the meaning of English words most of the time during their exposure to language learning. On the other hand, the result of the study shows that students also use some other applications for language practice such as Duolingo and Voscreen, in which users are being exposed to language quizzes with multiple-choice and fill-in-the blank items. Some interactive language practicing environments were also preferred by prep school students and this shows that rather than practicing book-based exercises, students seeks interactivity in the form of question and answer, and chatting with friends in other cultures.

RQ5. Design suggestions for mobile application regarding language learning

The results of the study showed that students mostly seek and demand vocabulary practicing applications, which should be more effective and useful. Furthermore, students stressed practicing collocations and listening practice. In addition to all of these, students showed that they are more likely to prefer learning and practicing English language in entertaining applications/environments such as gaming, chatting and competing. Therefore, it is important to consider interactivity and entertainment by gaming or contests in order to keep students engaged in such language learning environments.

In line with the findings of the study, it can be claimed that students effectively use their mobile devices to practice vocabulary by looking at online dictionary websites and applications. This gives a clue to designers of language learning mobile applications that vocabulary practice is the most needed issue by language learners. To do that, a mobile application in design and development stage should involve everything about vocabulary practice such as meanings of the words, collocations of words, pronunciation of words, and their use in sample sentences. Furthermore, findings of the study also showed that students can engage in language quiz shows that involve different quiz types as multiple-choice, fill-in-the blanks, matching, drag-and-drop items and translation questions after watching or listening to short conversations collected from different films, series and TV programs. Therefore, the main issue which should be addressed by designers in terms of language learning is vocabulary and translation. Since entertainment and interactivity were also emphasized by students, designers of such mobile language learning environments should also take these suggestions into consideration. For future research, scholars may involve participants from other universities or the same age group of English language learners to compare the results of this study, in particular in light of students' tendency toward mobile device use regarding English language learning. Furthermore, a follow-up study or a systematic review study analyzing studies covering a variety of contexts may also be conducted to see if the trend revealed from the current study is general.

Author Contributions: Data Analysis, C.Y.; Writing—original draft, S.Ö.; Writing—review and editing, S.Ö.

funding: This research received no external funding.

Acknowledgments: Thanks to school personnel for their valuable contribution during data collection.

Conflicts of Interest: The authors declare no conflict of interest.

References

1. Faille, M.; Morrison, K. Rise of the Mobile Phone. *National Post.* 5 April 2013. Available online: http://news. nationalpost.com/2013/04/05/graphic-rise-of-the-mobile-phone/ (accessed on 20 April 2018).
2. Ally, M. Mobile learning: From research to practice to impact education. *Learn. Teach. High. Educ. Gulf Perspect.* **2013**, *10*, 1–10.
3. Kulendran, M.; Lim, M.; Laws, G.; Chow, A.; Nehme, J.; Darzi, A.; Purkayastha, S. Surgical smarthphone applications across different platforms: Their evaluation, uses, and users. *Surg. Innov.* **2014**, *21*, 427–440. [CrossRef] [PubMed]
4. Kukulska-Hulme, A.; Traxler, J. *Mobile Learning: A Handbook for Educators and Trainers*; Routledge: London, UK, 2005.
5. Al-Emran, M.; Elsherif, H.M.; Shaalan, K. Investigating attitudes towards to use of mobile learning in higher education. *Comput. Hum. Behav.* **2016**, *56*, 93–102. [CrossRef]
6. Matias, A.; Wolf, D.F. Engaging students in online courses through the use of mobile technology. *Cut.-Edge Technol. High. Educ.* **2013**, *6*, 115–142.
7. Nassuora, A.B. Students' acceptance of mobile learning for higher education in Saudi Arabia. *Am. Acad. Sch. Res. J.* **2012**, *4*, 24–30. [CrossRef]
8. Caudill, J.G. The growth of m-learning and the growth of mobile computing: Parallel developments. *Int. Rev. Res. Open Distance Learn.* **2007**, *8*. [CrossRef]
9. Davis, J.S.; Garcia, G.D.; Wyckoff, M.M.; Alsafran, S.; Graygo, J.M.; Withum, K.F.; Shulman, C.I. Use of mobile learning module improves skills in chest tube insertion. *J. Surg. Res.* **2012**, *177*, 21–26. [CrossRef] [PubMed]
10. Kukulska-Hulme, A.; Traxler, J. Learning Design with Mobile and Wireless Technologies. In *Rethinking Pedagogy for the Digital Age*; Beetham, H., Sharpe, R., Eds.; Routledge: London, UK, 2007; pp. 180–192.
11. Shudong, W.; Higgins, M. Limitations of mobile phone learning. In Proceedings of the IEEE International Workshop on Wireless and Mobile Technologies in Education (WMTE 2005), Tokushima, Japan, 28–30 November 2005.
12. Iqbal, S.; Qureshi, I.A. M-Learning adoption: A perspective from a developing country. *Int. Rev. Res. Open Distance Learn.* **2012**, *13*, 147–164. [CrossRef]
13. Kukulska-Hulme, A.; Shield, L. An overview of mobile assisted language learning: From content delivery to supported collaboration and interaction. *ReCALL* **2008**, *20*, 271–289. [CrossRef]

14. Milrad, M.; Jackson, M. Designing and implementing educational mobile services in university classrooms using smart phones and cellular networks. *Int. J. Eng. Educ.* **2008**, *24*, 84–91.
15. Stockwell, G. Using mobile phones for vocabulary activities: Examining the effect of the platform. *Lang. Learn. Technol.* **2010**, *14*, 95–110.
16. Walker, R. "I don't think I would be where I am right now". Pupil perspectives on using mobile devices for learning. *Res. Learn. Technol.* **2013**. [CrossRef]
17. Dashtestani, R. Moving bravely towards mobile learning: Iranian students' use of mobile devices for learning English as a foreign language. *Comput. Assist. Lang. Learn.* **2015**, *29*, 815–832. [CrossRef]
18. Kinash, S.; Brand, J.; Mathew, T. Challenging mobile learning discourse through research: Student perceptions of Blackboard Mobile Learn and iPads. *Australas. J. Educ. Technol.* **2012**, *28*, 639–655. [CrossRef]
19. Traxler, J. *Mobile Learning for Languages: Can the Past Speak to the Future?* The International Research Foundation for English Language Education: Monterey, CA, USA, 2013; Available online: https://www.tirfonline.org/wp-content/uploads/2013/11/TIRF_MALL_Papers_Traxler.pdf (accessed on 20 April 2018).
20. Ogata, H.; Yano, Y. Knowledge awareness for computer-assisted language learning using hand-helds. *Int. J. Learn. Technol.* **2005**, *5*, 435–449.
21. Ardies, J.; De Maeyer, S.; Gijbels, D.; van Keulen, H. Students' attitudes towards technology. *Int. J. Technol. Des. Educ.* **2014**, 1–23. [CrossRef]
22. Creswell, J.W. *Educational Research: Planning, Conducting and Evaluating Quantitative and Qualtiative Research*; Pearson: London, UK, 2012.
23. Çelik, A. M-Learning attitude scale: Validity and realiability analyses. *J. Res. Educ. Teach.* **2013**, *4*, 172–185.
24. Cavus, N. Investigating mobile devices and LMS integration in higher education: Student perspectives. *Procedia Comput. Sci.* **2011**, *3*, 1469–1474. [CrossRef]
25. Wang, Y.S.; Wu, M.C.; Wang, H.Y. Investigating the determinants and age and gender differences in the acceptance of mobile learning. *Br. J. Educ. Technol.* **2009**, *40*, 92. [CrossRef]
26. Yang, S.H. Exploring college students' attitudes and self-efficacy of mobile learning. *Turk. Online J. Educ. Technol.* **2012**, *11*, 148.
27. Uzunboylu, H.; Cavus, N.; Ercag, E. Using mobile learning to increase environmental awareness. *Comput. Educ.* **2009**, *52*, 381–389. [CrossRef]
28. Motiwalla, L.F. Mobile learning: A framework and evaluation. *Comput. Educ.* **2007**, *49*, 581–596. [CrossRef]
29. Rees, H.; Noyes, J.M. Mobile telephones, computers and the Internet: Sex differences in adolescents' use and attitudes. *Cyber Psychol. Behav.* **2007**, *10*, 482–484. [CrossRef] [PubMed]
30. Khaddage, F.; Knezek, G. iLearn via mobile technology: A comparison of mobile learning attitudes among university students in two nations. In Proceedings of the IEEE 13th International Conference on Advanced Learning Technologies (ICALT), Beijing, China, 15–18 July 2013; pp. 256–258.
31. Taleb, Z.; Sohrabi, A. Learning on the move: The use of mobile technology to support learning for university students. *Procedia-Soc. Behav. Sci.* **2012**, *69*, 1102–1109. [CrossRef]
32. Skog, B. Mobiles and the Norwegian teen: Identity, gender, and class. In *Perpetual Contact: Mobile Communication, Private Talk, Public Performance*; Katz, J.E., Aakhus, M.A., Eds.; Cambridge University Press: Cambridge, UK, 2002; pp. 255–273.
33. Campbell, S.W. Perceptions of Mobile Phones in College Classrooms: Ringing, Cheating, and Classroom Policies. *Commun. Educ.* **2006**, *55*, 280–294. [CrossRef]
34. Chen, B.; Denoyelles, A. Exploring Students' Mobile Learning Practices in Higher Education. Educause Review Online. Available online: https://er.educause.edu/articles/2013/10/exploring-students-mobile-learning-practices-in-higher-education (accessed on 20 April 2018).
35. Al-Fahad, F.N. Students' attitudes and perceptions towards the effectiveness of mobile learning in King Said University, Saudi Arabia. *Turki. Online J. Educ. Technol.* **2009**, *8*, 111–119.

Article

The Role of Subjective Quality Judgements in User Preferences for Mobile Learning Apps

Maria Uther [1,*] and Sari Ylinen [2,3]

[1] Department of Psychology, University of Wolverhampton, Wolverhampton WV1 1LY, UK
[2] Faculty of Educational Sciences, University of Helsinki, P.O. Box 9, 00014 Helsinki, Finland;
   sari.ylinen@helsinki.fi
[3] Department of Psychology and Logopedics, Faculty of Medicine, University of Helsinki, P.O. Box 63,
   00014 Helsinki, Finland
* Correspondence: m.uther@wlv.ac.uk

Received: 20 November 2018; Accepted: 18 December 2018; Published: 24 December 2018

Abstract: This study investigated whether subjective quality judgements on sound and picture quality across three devices (iPhone, iPad, and iPad mini) affected user preferences for learning applications. We tested 20 native Finnish-speaking users trialing generic audio clips, video clips, and two kinds of learning apps that were heavily reliant on sound. It was found that there was a main effect of the device on perceived sound quality, replicating earlier findings. However, these judgements did not impact on the users' preferences for different devices nor on their preferences for different applications. The results are interpreted as indicating that perceived quality and affordances are less important for users in these contexts than other considerations (e.g., convenience, mobility, etc.).

Keywords: mobile learning; audio interaction; subjective perception

---

1. Introduction

The field of 'mobile learning' initially grew from the field of e-learning, as applied to the use of mobile phones to develop applications for learning, rather than to that of non-portable personal computers (PC) (note: the term 'mobile learning' is not used to denote a special kind of learning, but rather to describe learning that is supported by use of mobile devices). Mobile phones were thought to be advantageous for learning in several ways, e.g., portability, mobility, potential for location-based services, etc. (see [1–8] for a review). However, there were other ways in which mobile phones were deemed to offer advantages over fixed PC-based learning. For example, Uther [8] highlighted the potential of mobile phones in terms of 'affordances' for audio interaction. For example, as a phone is built for speaking and listening it may lend itself to superior implementation of audio-based applications. Since those early days, there has been further development of technology such that the term 'mobile learning' now encompasses a myriad of small, portable devices (e.g., small and large tablets and, more recently, 'phablet'-type devices). The boundary between 'phone' and mobile devices has become far more blurred.

The exploration of learner experiences with different mobile devices (phones versus tablets) is of interest as it is clear that the use of handheld devices (especially mobiles) for learning is on the rise [1]. On the other hand, mobile phones have appeared to educators less suited to pedagogical use compared to larger screen devices [9]. This is of course likely due to the fact that perception of what suits 'learning' from a teacher's point of view is necessarily going to entail visual content, whereas, for some fields (e.g., language or musical learning), the reliance on visual content is not as important, and the natural 'affordance' of the necessary device should be anchored more towards the device's capability in terms of audio content delivery. The concept of affordance is critical to the learning outcomes and is discussed in more detail in references [10,11] for example.

This study builds on previous studies [10,12] that explored affordance of phones versus tablets for learning applications that heavily used sound. Those studies highlighted differences in user perceptions of sound quality, which may in turn impact on the learning and user experience. The first study by Uther and Banks [10] found that sound quality was perceived to be different for different device types (smartphone versus tablet) even when physical acoustical qualities were controlled for. At that time, generic audio clips were perceived as being inferior in quality when delivered on a phone as compared to a tablet. On the other hand, research done a few years later [12] showed somewhat different trends, with phones rating higher in perceived sound quality compared to tablets. The discrepancy between the different studies was attributed to the different positioning in terms of markets for phones and smartphones in the intervening years (smartphones were much more ubiquitous in 2017 than in 2013 when testing was done). The earlier study investigated the perceived sound quality of different English-language learning apps and, although they examined first-language (L1) and second-language (L2) speakers of English, that study used L2 speakers that were already quite experienced in English as they were living in the UK and used the language on a daily basis.

This study sought to extend the previous studies by investigating the importance of perceived sound quality judgements for mobile learning applications that use sound in a non-UK sample. Unlike the previous studies, this study contrasted perceptions of both music and language learning applications within the same study and also used a more naïve group of L2 speakers of English (those living in Finland). This latter manipulation was important as we felt it was important to determine whether sound quality judgements of words were determined by language background. In a previous study with children [13] using a speech-training application [14], it was found that non-native speech samples were related more poorly. Hence, the following hypotheses were formulated in relation to this study:

H1: That Finnish speakers might rate sound quality of the English language content more poorly compared to any Finnish language content.

H2: That there would be a difference in perception of sound quality between phone and tablet categories of devices.

H3: That the sound quality might affect users' rating of the likelihood of future use as well as suitability of the device to the application.

2. Materials and Methods

2.1. Participants

Twenty participants (15 female, 5 males, mean age 30 years, age range between 22 and 53 years) were recruited from the University of Helsinki via email distribution lists and social media. The sample consisted primarily of employed individuals and included seven graduate students. Out of all participants, only nine owned an iPhone (the rest owned other brands of smartphones). We did not have to exclude any participants as a result of diagnosed or possibly undiagnosed hearing impairments in our screening questionnaire. One participant out of 20 owned an iPad mini and five participants out of 20 owned an iPad, with one participant owning an Android tablet. In accordance with ethical guidelines, the participants gave written informed consent and were given a free movie ticket worth approximately €10 for their time. They were free to withdraw at any time without penalty.

2.2. Stimuli and materials

The study used mobile devices which had identical sound output capabilities and similar user interface and interaction styles. These were: an iPhone version 6s, an iPad mini 4, and an iPad Air 2. The mobile devices were also loaded with the Learn English App (produced by the British Council) and the Auralia Pitch Trainer App.

In order to keep the sound output constant across devices, a pair of Bose Bluetooth headphones was used. In addition, a sound level meter measured the peak, mean and range of the generic sound samples played (which were normalized in advance using audio editing software). This was done to calibrate the ranges of the stimuli to an approximately equal level using the recorded decibel levels.

We used several questionnaires derived from [10,12]. There were general demographic, language, and musical training background questionnaires. These questionnaires gathered data about age, gender, mobile device ownership, language background, and musical training background. There were also questionnaires from the work of Uther & Banks [10] on sensory and cognitive affordances, which rated the users' perception of sound and picture quality on a seven-point scale rating from best to worst. These scales for sound quality were developed with the International Telecommunication Union standards ITU-R BS.1284-1 [15] in mind. Those standards recommend listener grading scales from 'Bad' to 'Excellent.' A7, rather than a five-point scale of rating, was also chosen, as it has been shown to better map the configural space of participant perceptions [16].

2.3. Design

The study was run as a 'mixed' design, with musical training as group factor. Using the questionnaire data, the participants were categorized as: (1) non-musicians, (2) amateur musicians with no formal training but some occasional musical practice, and (3) musicians with formal musical training (e.g., passed accredited music exams). The subject factors included device type (iPad, iPad mini, or iPhone), media type (music, audiobook, or video), and training type (music versus language training app).

2.4. Procedure

The participants were given an informed consent and a participant information sheet before the session started. They were then given the demographic, language, and music background questionnaires. The participants then completed a set of pre-defined tasks on each device (iPhone, iPad mini, and iPad), with the order of presentation of each task on each device randomized. They first rated generic sound and video quality on each device (as an index of sensory affordance). To test sound quality, two audio samples were played: (1) A standardized 15 second passage from the audio-book 'No.1 Lady's Detective Agency' (2) A standardized 15 second musical sample from Yo-Yo Ma's rendition of Bach's Cello Suite #1 in G. They were also given two word-lists of the same words in their native Finnish language and non-native English to rate for sound quality. To rate video quality, a short, 15 second sample of a high-definition video of the same audio musical piece (Bach Cello Suite #1 in G) being performed was played. The participants' headphones were kept in a constant position throughout the testing session and across all devices. The participants filled in a questionnaire to give ratings as they heard each sound.

The participants were then asked to use one of two mobile learning applications for a few minutes. Following this, they were asked to rate the audio and video quality as well as the perceived suitability of each device being used for each software application and the likelihood that they would use that application on a seven-point scale, as in references [10,12]. Finally, the participants were also asked to rank each device (iPhone, iPad mini, and iPad) according to which they felt would give the best sound quality. When asked this question, they were allowed to give 'same' rankings to two or three devices at once. The whole experiment took no more than 30 min.

3. Results

We first compared the subjective ratings of audio and picture quality of generic samples across iPad, iPad mini, and iPhone as an index of sensory affordances [10]. For audio quality, three types of sound were rated for user-perceived quality (audio book, music sample, or audio portion of the video clip playing the same piece of music as the audio clip). The data were analyzed with repeated measures ANOVA using device type and stimulus type as within-subject factors. We also analyzed the group factor of musical proficiency. The analyses for generic content quality rating were performed separately from the application rating, and Bonferroni corrections for family-wise error rates were applied for pairwise multiple comparisons.

There was only a main effect of device type on audio rating, with the iPhone having a lower sound quality rating compared to the iPad mini or iPad ($F_{(1,19)} = 6.333$, $p < 0.05$; see Figure 1 below). Post-hoc Bonferroni-corrected pairwise comparisons showed that there was no statistically significant difference between the iPad mini and iPad devices.

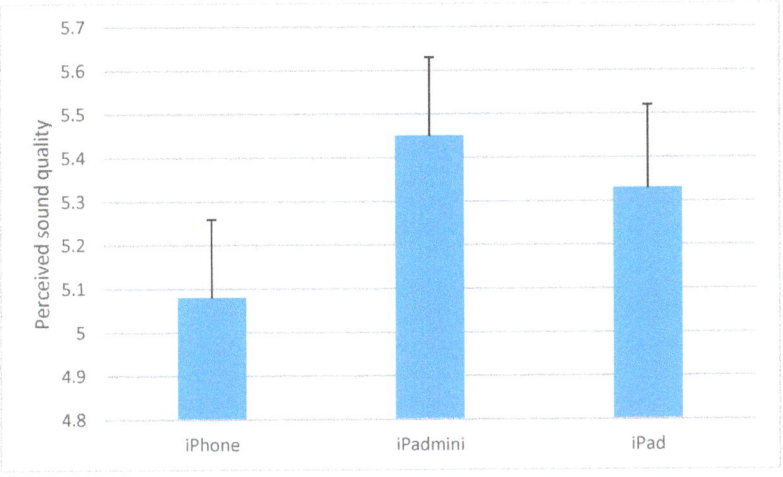

Figure 1. Mean perceived sound quality for generic content as a function of device type.

Further multivariate analyses of other measures did not show any statistically significant different results between different application types (musical training versus language training) nor device type interactions. In general, the applications were rated relatively high (mean rating between 5.5 and 5.0 on a Likert scale of 1–7), but by contrast, the likelihood of future use ratings was much more modest (mean between 3.6 and 4.0 on a Likert scale of 1–7). The latter modest ratings likely reflect the fact that there was little use for the applications, especially—as most participants noticed—because they found the applications too basic for their needs. There were also no significant differences in perceived sound quality between different language stimuli (native versus non-native).

4. Discussion

In this study, we addressed three hypotheses. Our first hypothesis was that Finnish speakers might rate the sound quality of English language speech more poorly compared to native language speech. This hypothesis was not supported. We were surprised as this contrasted with data from another study using a different language learning application with children who were Finnish speakers of English [13]. The contrast in findings between the two Finnish studies could be due to the fact that this sample was already fairly proficient compared to the child sample we tested in the other study. Even though the stimuli were the same, it was clear that the adults in this study had language proficiency that was better than that of the children in the other study. Indeed, the participants here had universally learned English from about age nine to adulthood, so there were very clear differences in the level of English proficiency. In order to see similar patterns as we did with the child sample, we will likely need to test adult participants with a lower level of proficiency to match the child sample. Another possibility is that children cannot tell the difference between difficulties caused by sound quality and those due to their own (poor) non-native language skills, whereas the adults might better realize that their difficulties are due to their skills and not to sound quality. In this sense, adults may be more objective in their sound quality judgements.

With respect to the second hypothesis regarding the perceived sound quality using different devices, the pattern of data here was somewhat different from that found in the most recent study by our lab [12] with a UK-based sample. On the other hand, the pattern of results was more similar to that found in the first study [10]. These differences could be because the market penetration of Apple devices is different for the United Kingdom compared to Finland. One analysis showed that UK mobile users used iOS more than Android, whereas the reverse was true for Finland [17]. This was also supported by the fact that there were very few iPad users within the sample (n = 5) and also fewer iPhone users (n = 8). Although device brand did not appear to affect the ratings, the small sample of iOS tablet users might not be large enough to reflect any real effects. Still, the most likely explanation for the discrepancy with more recent findings is that iPads were rated primarily by non-users—and so they might have been perceived as 'better' if, for example, they are perceived as superior products (e.g., because of their price, which might be out of the users' reach). It is important to note that the mobile devices compared here differed in price and market position, which might be the most likely cause of the perceived differences. This is not unlike the effects seen in other contexts of sound quality tests, where branding appeared to affect users' ratings [18,19].

Finally, the last hypothesis that sound quality might affect the users' impressions of suitability and future use was not supported. The data clearly showed that despite perceived differences, this did not appear to affect the learners' perception of suitability of a learning application for a particular device nor their desire to use such an application in the future. Any ratings on attributes such as suitability or sound quality did not impact on the likelihood of using the learning application. Taken in the context of the field of mobile learning, this is an interesting finding as it suggests that learners may opt for convenience of use as a primary criterion for the selection of an application [20]. Despite the fact that the implementation of mobile learning applications is not without challenges or even negatives from a learner [21,22] or even teacher perspective [9], mobile devices have an appeal for affording portability, collaboration, and 'just-in-time' interaction. In terms of future research, although it is important to examine device and learner interactions as we have done here, we also need to examine the extent to which mobile learning is adopted in contexts characterized by specific socio-cultural factors which have been argued to be critical for the successful implementation of mobile learning applications [23].

5. Conclusions

In summary, it appears that sound quality is not tied to purely physical qualities, as was found in other studies. Moreover, users perceive sound differences between devices even when none exists. In terms of the central focus of this study regarding mobile learning, the extent to which subjective differences in sound-quality experience impact on the actual learning outcomes is not directly determined by this study. In all likelihood, the factors examined do not appear to be driving consumer choices and overall impressions of suitability. Future research may, for example, use a different approach (e.g., using qualitative measures) to examine in more detail the extent to which differences in subjective experiences are affected by aspects such as branding, previous experience, etc. More importantly, determining the order of priority of features for the user (e.g., portability, affordance for collaboration, etc.) is also critical for the successful planning of mobile learning applications. However, only further studies with larger samples and tied to actual learning outcomes will be capable of determining the impact of different factors on educational outcomes.

Author Contributions: Conceptualization, M.U. and S.Y., methodology, M.U., S.Y., statistical analysis, M.U., writing, original draft preparation, M.U., writing—review & editing, S.Y.

funding: This research was funded by the Nokia Foundation Visiting Professor Grant awarded to Professor Uther for a visit to Cicero Learning, University of Helsinki, Finland in 2018.

Acknowledgments: The authors acknowledge the assistance of Mari Tervaniemi in practical matters related to accommodating and hosting Uther's research visit to Finland. The authors also acknowledge the assistance of Anna-Riikka Smolander of the University of Helsinki in relation to participant recruitment.

Conflicts of Interest: The authors declare no conflict of interests.

References

1. Wu, W.H.; Wu, Y.C.J.; Chen, C.Y.; Kao, H.Y.; Lin, C.H.; Huang, S.H. Review of trends from mobile learning studies: A meta-analysis. *Comput. Educ.* **2012**, *59*, 817–827. [CrossRef]

2. Kukulska-Hulme, A. Mobile usability in educational contexts: What have we learnt? *Int. Rev. Res. Open Distance Learn.* **2007**, *8*, 1–16. [CrossRef]

3. Orr, G. A review of literature in mobile learning: Affordances and constraints. In Proceedings of the 6th IEEE International Conference on Wireless, Mobile and Ubiquitous Technologies in Education, Kaohsiung, Taiwan, 12–16 April 2010; pp. 107–111.

4. Jacob, S.M.; Issac, B. The Mobile Devices and its Mobile Learning Usage Analysis. In Proceedings of the International Multiconference of Engineers and Computer Scientists, Hong Kong, China, 19–21 March 2008; Volume I.

5. Sung, Y.T.; Chang, K.E.; Liu, T.C. The effects of integrating mobile devices with teaching and learning on students' learning performance: A meta-analysis and research synthesis. *Comput. Educ.* **2016**, *94*, 252–275. [CrossRef]

6. Sharples, M.; Pea, R. Mobile learning. In *The Cambridge Handbook of the Learning Sciences*, 2nd ed.; Sawyer, R.K., Ed.; Cambridge University Press: New York, NY, USA, 2015; pp. 501–521.

7. Koole, M.; Buck, R.; Anderson, K.; Laj, D. A Comparison of the Uptake of Two Research Models in Mobile Learning: The FRAME Model and the 3-Level Evaluation Framework. *Educ. Sci.* **2018**, *8*, 114. [CrossRef]

8. Uther, M. Mobile Internet usability: What can 'mobile learning' learn from the past? In *Proceedings—IEEE International Workshop on Wireless and Mobile Technologies in Education*; IEEE Computer Society: Washington, DC, USA, 2002; pp. 174–176.

9. Şad, S.N.; Göktaş, Ö. Preservice teachers' perceptions about using mobile phones and laptops in education as mobile learning tools. *Br. J. Educ. Technol.* **2014**, *45*, 606–618. [CrossRef]

10. Uther, M.; Banks, A.P. The influence of affordances on user preferences for multimedia language learning applications. *Behav. Inf. Technol.* **2016**, *35*, 277–289. [CrossRef]

11. Hartson, R. Cognitive, physical, sensory, and functional affordances in interaction design. *Behav. Inf. Technol.* **2003**, *22*, 315–338. [CrossRef]

12. Uther, M.; Banks, A.P. User Perceptions of Sound Quality: Implications for the Design and Use of Audio-Based Mobile Applications. *Int. J. Hum. Comput. Interact.* **2018**. [CrossRef]

13. Uther, M.; Smolander, A.-R.; Junttila, K.; Kurimo, M.; Karhila, R.; Enarvi, S.; Ylinen, S. User Experiences from L2 Children Using a Speech Learning Application: Implications for Developing Speech Training Applications for Children. *Adv. Hum.-Comput. Interact.* **2018**, *2018*, 7345397.

14. Karhila, R.; Ylinen, S.; Enarvi, S.; Palomäki, K.; Nikulin, A.; Rantula, O.; Viitanen, V.; Dhinakaran, K.; Smolander, A.-R.; Kallio, H.; et al. SIAK—A Game for Foreign Language Pronunciation Learning. In *Interspeech 2017*; ISCA: Stockholm, Sweden, 2017.

15. International Telecommunications Union. *General Methods for the Subjective Assessment of Sound Quality*; International Telecommunications Union: Geneva, Switzerland, 2003.

16. Maxell, M.S.; Jacoby, J. Is there an optimal number of alternatives for likert-scale items? Effects of testing time and scale properties. *J. Appl. Psychol.* **1972**, *56*, 506–509.

17. DeviceAtlas. Android v iOS Market Share 2018. 2018. Available online: https://deviceatlas.com/blog/android-v-ios-market-share (accessed on 21 December 2018).

18. Toole, F.E.; Olive, S.E. Hearing is Believing vs. Believing is Hearing: Blind vs. Sighted Listening Tests, and Other Interesting Things. In *Audio Engineering Society 97th Convention*; AES: San Francisco, CA, USA, 1994.

19. Beresford, K.; Ford, N.; Rumsey, F.; Zielinski, S. Contextual effects on sound quality judgements: Listening room and automotive environments. In *Audio Engineering Society 120th Convention*; Audio Engineering Society: Paris, France, 2006.

20. Chang, C.C.; Yan, C.F.; Tseng, J.S. Perceived convenience in an extended technology acceptance model: Mobile technology and English learning for college students. *Australas. J. Educ. Technol.* **2012**, *28*, 809–826. [CrossRef]

21. Heflin, H.; Shewmaker, J.; Nguyen, J. Impact of mobile technology on student attitudes, engagement, and learning. *Comput. Educ.* **2017**, *107*, 91–99. [CrossRef]

22. Chu, H.C. Potential negative effects of mobile learning on students' learning achievement and cognitive load-a format assessment perspective. *Educ. Technol. Soc.* **2013**, *17*, 332–344. [CrossRef]

23. Koole, M.L. A model for framing mobile learning. *Mob. Learn. Transform. Deliv. Educ. Train.* **2009**, *1*, 25–47. [CrossRef]

Review

A Comparison of the Uptake of Two Research Models in Mobile Learning: The FRAME Model and the 3-Level Evaluation Framework

Marguerite Koole [1,*], Rosemary Buck [2], Kerry Anderson [3] and Drea Laj [4]

1   Department of Curriculum Studies, College of Education, University of Saskatchewan,
     Saskatoon, SK S7N 5B5, Canada

2   Calgary Board of Education, University of Saskatchewan, Saskatoon, SK S7N 5B5, Canada;
     reb860@mail.usask.ca

3   Saskatoon Public Schools, University of Saskatchewan, Saskatoon, SK S7N 5B5, Canada;
     kaa946@mail.usask.ca

4   Nanaimo-Ladysmith Public Schools, University of Saskatchewan, Saskatoon, SK S7N 5B5, Canada;
     anl634@mail.usask.ca

*   Correspondence: m.koole@usask.ca; Tel.: +1-306-966-7638

Received: 16 June 2018; Accepted: 2 August 2018; Published: 7 August 2018

Abstract: This paper discusses the diffusion of two models of mobile learning within the educational research literature: The Framework for the Rational Analysis of Mobile Learning (FRAME) model and the 3-Level Evaluation Framework (3-LEF). The main purpose is to analyse how the two models, now over 10 years old, have been referenced in the literature and applied in research. The authors conducted a systematic review of publications that referenced the seminal papers that originally introduced the models. The research team summarized the publications by recording the abstracts and documenting how the models were cited, described, interpreted, selected, rejected, and/or modified. The summaries were then coded according to criteria such as fields of study, reasons for use, criticisms and modifications. In total, 208 publications referencing the FRAME model and 97 publications referencing the 3-LEF were included. Of these, 55 publications applied the FRAME model and 10 applied the 3-LEF in research projects. The paper concludes that these two models/frameworks were likely chosen for reasons other than philosophical commensurability. Additional studies of the uptake of other mobile learning models is recommended in order to develop an understanding of how mobile learning, as a field, is progressing theoretically.

Keywords: mobile learning; FRAME model; 3-level evaluation framework; diffusion of models; systematic review

1. Introduction

Mobile learning came into focus in the 1990s as personal digital assistants (PDAs) and, later, mobile phones began to facilitate learning [1]. In 2005, *m-learning* became an accepted term [1], although the definition of the term remained problematic. Within this relatively short time span, researchers and practitioners have grappled with defining, understanding, designing, applying, and evaluating mobile learning. They question who and what is mobile as well as how to integrate mobile tools into pedagogical practices. Conceptual models and frameworks play a significant role in answering these questions because they explain "either graphically or in narrative form, the main things to be studied—the key factors, concepts, or variables—and the presumed relationships among them" [2]. Evaluation models are also significant tools; they can be formative (information about the mobile intervention/tool is fed back to the researchers for improvement during the learning experience), summative (information is used to judge the usefulness of the intervention/tool after the learning experience), or both [3].

The purpose of this paper is to examine the uptake of two m-learning frameworks: Koole's Framework for the Rational Analysis of Mobile Learning (FRAME) conceptual framework [4,5] and Vavoula and Sharples' 3-level evaluation framework (3-LEF) as designed for the MyArt Space project [6,7]. A preliminary examination of citation numbers in Google Scholar suggests that both models have been referenced extensively. As of writing this paper, the number of Google Scholar citations for the FRAME model [4,5] is over 500; the number for the 3-LEF [6,7] is over 300. Upon closer examination, these numbers are somewhat misleading because they include any kind of reference—even references that appear in reference lists without having cited the original papers within the body text. Furthermore, the numbers from sources such as Google Scholar and other common indices fail to provide information about how the models have been used, if they have been understood and/or interpreted accurately, if they have offered a springboard to innovation in mobile learning, or if they have stimulated the emergence of other models.

A closer examination of how and why models proliferate through the field of mobile learning (and beyond) may help us gain a sense of the assumptions and perspectives of the researchers who have referenced the models. A general criticism of the field of educational technology is that there is insufficient evidence of critical thinking in the development of new perspectives, paradigms, methodologies, and reflective practice [8]. According to Yanchar, Gibbons, Gabbitas, and Matthews [8], critical thinking refers to "a cloud of intellectual processes by which ideas and processes are formulated, expressed, examined, questioned, tested, proven, discussed, and used within a field." So, if authors have selected or rejected a model, did they have any underlying philosophical, practical, or operational reasons? If researchers fail to base their selection upon critically-thought-out criteria, what are the implications for the field? How can we determine "the conditions for progress" in the field [9]?

In order to examine the uptake of the FRAME and 3-LEF, the researchers conducted a systematic review of publications that cited the seminal articles in which Koole, Vavoula, and Sharples introduced their frameworks. The publications were summarized, the reference and citation information were documented, the abstracts were recorded, and any specific comments pertaining to the frameworks were recorded. These notes were then coded according to a list of criteria such as fields of study and/or researchers that have cited the models and their reasons for adoption or rejection.

This paper will first describe the two models. Then, the authors will explain the rationale for the study. The methodology section describes the databases, search terms, inclusion criteria, and exclusion criteria. The results section provides both numeric data of the included publications (number, types, geographic reach, topics of research, and research methods) and qualitative data (on reasons for use, critiques, and modifications of the models). The paper concludes by noting that there is need to trace the diffusion of theoretical models in order to understand the extent to which epistemological and ontological positions are guiding research in mobile learning, and more broadly, educational technology.

2. The Models

As mentioned above, the primary articles in which the models were introduced were published in between 2006 and 2009 [4–7]. These two models were chosen because they were developed and published at approximately the same time. These models are also over 10 years old; therefore, sufficient time has elapsed, and our research team can trace referencing patterns. These two models were also selected because the researchers are most familiar with them, which helped the team examine how the models were being used and (mis-)understood. Although, both the FRAME and the 3-LEF can be used outside of mobile learning, they can be applied to other educational technologies (including non-digital technologies). The 3-LEF is specifically an evaluative framework that outlines phases in the evaluation process. The FRAME can be used in an evaluative way, but it is more of a conceptual model in that it aids in the conceptualization of how phenomena are articulated.

2.1. The FRAME Model

The FRAME model was developed for a master's thesis [4] at a time when mobile learning was first entering the mainstream of educational research. The purpose of the thesis was to examine key characteristics of a collection of mobile devices within the context of distance education at the post-secondary level. The study began in 2004 when few other mobile-learning models and frameworks were available. The master's thesis was made available online in 2006. A chapter was published in 2009 in a free, open-access book, which likely aided in the proliferation of the model worldwide [10]; this open-access chapter is the document that is primarily referenced in the literature.

Originally, Koole worked primarily within a constructivist perspective, but also drew upon cognitivist theories (such as [11–14]). Special interest was placed upon situated learning (such as [15,16]), human-computer interaction (such as [17–19]), and classics in distance education (such as [20,21]). Koole has since moved to a sociomaterialist view of the FRAME model [22], which takes an ontological perspective in which the human and the material are equally important.

The FRAME Venn diagram depicts the three main aspects that influence and co-produce mobile learning (Figure 1). Within a researcher-delimited context, the key aspects of the FRAME model comprise the device, learner, and social aspects. The FRAME model requires a basic understanding of set theory, a branch of mathematical logic. In a Venn diagram, no one part is more or less important than any other. In the FRAME model, each circle is the same size symbolizing that they are equally important. Even the center of the circle (which is labelled "mobile learning:) is no more or less important than the parts that come together to create it nor is any other part of the diagram more important than the context within which it is situated (the "information context"). The reason the Venn diagram was used was to depict the pieces that come together co-construct the phenomenon of mobile learning. Logically, then, it is not possible to suggest that the FRAME model is device-centric, technologically determinist, or socially determinist. Similar to a jigsaw puzzle, all the pieces are necessary to create the finished picture, but no piece is more important than any other. The whole is just as important as the parts.

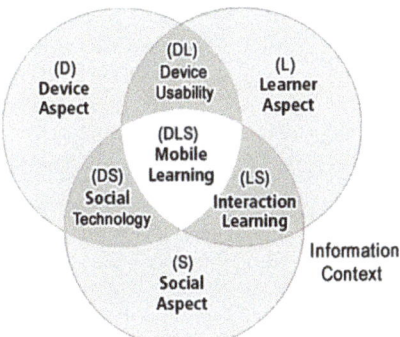

Figure 1. The Framework for the Rational Analysis of Mobile Learning (FRAME) model.

The device, learner, and social aspects overlap with each other creating the interaction-learning, social-technology, and device-usability intersections. The center of the Venn diagram shows the overlapping of all three aspects where mobile learning emerges. The overlapping of the circles guided the development of a list of key questions [5] that designers could use in developing mobile learning environments and interventions. Table 1 summarizes the key (but partial) characteristics of each part of the FRAME model.

Table 1. Elements of the FRAME Model.

Set/Intersection	Characteristics
Information context	Where learning occurs
Device aspect	Physical components Input/output capabilities File storage and retrieval Processor speed Error rates
Learner aspect	Prior knowledge Memory Context and transfer Learning proclivities Emotions Motivation
Social Aspect	Conversation Cooperation Interaction
Device usability	Portability Information availability Psychological comfort Satisfaction
Social technology	Networking System connectivity Collaboration/interaction tools
Interaction learning	Interaction (learners, instructors, content, computers) Situated cognition Learning communities Pedagogical practices Curriculum
Mobile learning	Mediation, mediators, translators Information access and selection Knowledge navigation

2.2. The 3-Level Evaluation Framework (3-LEF)

The 3-LEF model emerged as research was being done on the Myartspace project [7]. Myartspace was a project in which mobile phones were used by children on a field trip to a museum. Using their phones, learners could collect information and send it to a website. The students could view, share and present the information they gathered; in this way, they could digitally connect their field trip artifacts to their classroom and home environments. Pedagogically, the project involved an inquiry learning approach in which the learners would formulate their own questions, design their own plans, and determine what they learned.

The potential and effectiveness of project was evaluated using the 3-LEF. Whilst maintaining a focus on the socio-cultural context of learning [6], the framework is highly structured and is based upon Meek's "lifecycle approach" [23]. The lifecycle approach was originally developed for a PhD dissertation in the field of software engineering. In this approach, evaluation occurs through the processes of conception, requirements analysis, design, implementation and deployment. The 3-LEF is sometimes referred to as the 3M framework because it comprises three levels: micro, meso, and macro. The micro level concerns the actual behaviours, interactions, and activities of the users. The meso level examines patterns in learning experiences across individuals and focuses on critical incidents—inclusive of both "breakthroughs and breakdowns" [6]. To identify gaps between what is expected and what actually occurs, the data collection occurs in three stages. Stage one involves collecting information through interviews with users and document analysis regarding expected and desired behaviours (of students and tools). In stage two, the researchers collect data through live observation or audio/video recordings, about what actually occurred. And, finally, in stage three, the researchers conduct reflective interviews with the users and analyse the data collected in stages one and two. To summarize, the 3-LEF combines three processes.

1. Development process phases: requirements analysis, design, implementation, and deployment.
2. Levels of granularity: micro, meso, and macro.
3. Stages of data collection and analysis: stage 1 documentation of expectations, stage 2 documentation of actual activities, and stage 3 of gap analysis.

In order to help visualize the process, the authors provide an analysis-and-evaluation diagram (Figure 2).

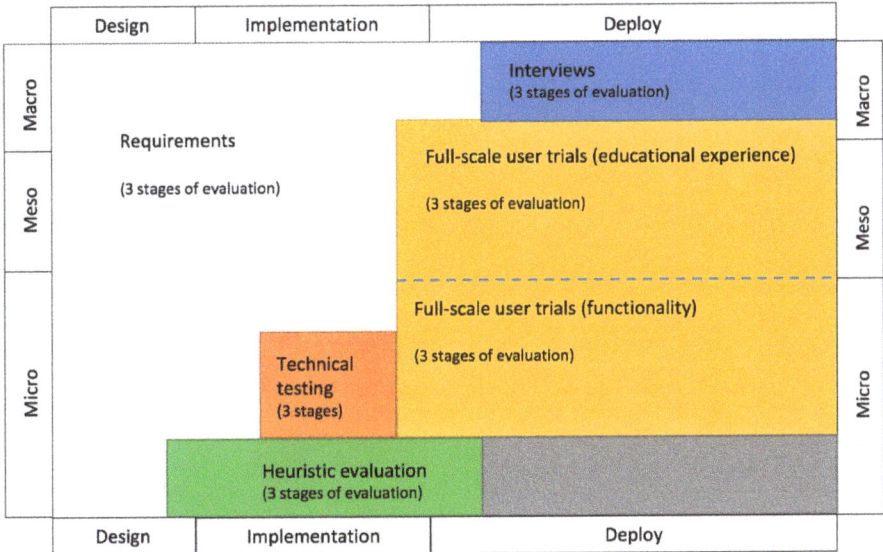

Figure 2. The 3-Level Evaluation Framework (3-LEF) evaluation and analysis process [7].

The original and more detailed version of Figure 2 appears in the Myartspace article [7]. Although the Myartspace article provides an example of how the framework was applied, the article on "meeting the challenges" [6] is more cited in the literature. The article [6] outlines six challenges in evaluating mobile learning, introduces the 3-LEF, how the framework was applied to the Myartspace project, and discusses how the six challenges were address through application of the 3-LEF.

2.3. Brief Comparison of the Two Models

Table 2 provides a summary of the main steps as *originally* intended by the authors of the FRAME and the 3-LEF models. (As will be discussed later, the models have been used in ways unpredicted by the authors.)

Table 2. Summary of the main features of both models (FRAME and 3-LEF).

	FRAME	3-LEF
Philosophy	Originally, social constructivist; shifted to sociomaterialist.	Socio-cultural.
Framework	Conceptual model; descriptive.	Evaluative model; procedural.
Implementation	Descriptive approach: Researcher can start at any section (context, aspects, intersections) in the Venn diagram; collect data on components that exist in each section; analyse how sections intersect.	Lifecycle approach to evaluation: researcher systematically studies the development process of a mobile tool at the micro, meso, and macro level of granularity.
Data collection	First order observation (direct observation/experience) or second order observation (interviews with users or examination of written documentation) of mobile learning situation, context, activities, and tools.	During each stage of development (conception, requirements analysis, design, implementation, and deployment), the researcher documents expectations and actual activities at each level of granularity.
Analysis	Analysis involves documentation of observations. Researcher writes a rich description of the mobile learning phenomenon.	Researcher conducts a gap analysis by comparing expectations to actual activities.

3. Motivation and Rationale for the Study

In their review of models and frameworks for designing mobile learning experiences and environments, Hsu and Ching [24] documented and categorized 17 notable models published between 2007 and 2015. (For the purposes of this paper, the terms *model* (*conceptual model*) and *framework* are used interchangeably. The differences between models and frameworks are outside the scope of this study.) A simple Google search will reveal that there are far more than 17; an exhaustive list needs yet to be compiled and published. Noting the proliferation of models and frameworks in the field of mobile learning, our research team began to question how existing models are being selected, extended, and/or rejected. We hoped that exploring the implementation and/or critiques of current models facilitate our understanding of how and why new models continue to emerge. Ultimately, what tools do mobile learning researchers require in order to answer their research questions? For these reasons, the main goals of this paper are to

- determine the number of references to the model/framework;
- examine the geographic and temporal reach of the model/framework;
- determine the number of times the model/framework has been used to guide research projects;
- locate the reasons why the model/framework was chosen;
- locate and analyse critiques of the model/framework (i.e., why the model/framework was rejected); and
- examine how the model/framework may have been modified.

4. Research Questions

Based on the aforementioned rationale and goals, the primary research questions are

- How have the seminal articles introducing the FRAME model and the 3-LEF been referenced in the education literature (including but not limited to the field of mobile learning)?
- How has the FRAME/3-LEF been used within the field of education?

5. Research Methodology

The research team for this project searched for any publication that cited the original ("seminal") articles introducing the FRAME model [4,5] and the 3-LEF [6,7], which were published since June 2006 and May 2018. The inclusion criteria were broad because our team was interested in the range of study designs, subject areas, and geographic range in which the models have been used. The publications included spanned those that referred to the seminal articles only in passing to those that discussed and/or applied the model/framework in depth. Publications were rejected if they made no substantive comments about the seminal articles or the model/framework (failed to cite the seminal articles within the body text). We excluded articles by Koole, Sharples, and Vavoula in which they self-cited the introductory articles.

Each member of the research team received training from a research librarian on selecting the databases and formulating search strings. The following databases and search mechanisms were accessed:

- Eric;
- USearch;
- Proquest;
- Web of Science;
- Google Scholar;
- Research Gate;
- Academia.edu;
- Google search engine.

Because the search was so specific, the list of key words was kept simple. Table 3 lists the key words used in the database searches.

Table 3. Keywords used in database searches.

FRAME Model	3-LEF
Koole	Vavoula and Sharples
FRAME model	3-level evaluation
Mobile learning	3-LEF
	Myartspace

The author names were necessary in all searches; otherwise, the number of results returned was overwhelming. For example, without "Koole" in a search for FRAME model, the results yielded were in excess of 17,000. Similarly, "Vavoula" and "Sharples" were used in all the searches for the 3-LEF.

As the publications were located, they were summarized, the reference and citation information were documented, the abstracts were recorded, and any specific comments pertaining to the frameworks were documented. Table 4 lists the information documented for each paper located.

Table 4. Template for summarizing publications.

Category	Notes
Author, date	Last name, date
Reference	APA citation
Country of author	Country
Country of research	Country
Type of research	Methodology, methods, approach
Applied	Yes/No
Summary	Description/abstract
Note	Notes about application, quality of references, observations, significant quotations.

The summaries were then coded in Nvivo according to a list of criteria (a priori coding) such as fields of study, and/or researchers that have cited the models and their reasons for adoption or rejection. (See Appendix A for a complete list of codes/nodes).

The "applied" code was important in allowing the researchers to run queries in Nvivo separating those studies in which the FRAME or 3-LEF were applied in research. This helped the research team to determine the extent to which the seminal articles were merely cited (code: "literature review") in contrast to the number of times the model/framework was actually used.

6. Results

6.1. Number of Publications Included in the Study

In total, 208 publications cited the FRAME model and 97 publications cited the 3-LEF. As can be seen in Figure 3, the FRAME model experienced its highest uptake in 2015. The 3-LEF diagram shows 2013 and 2015 as its years of highest uptake.

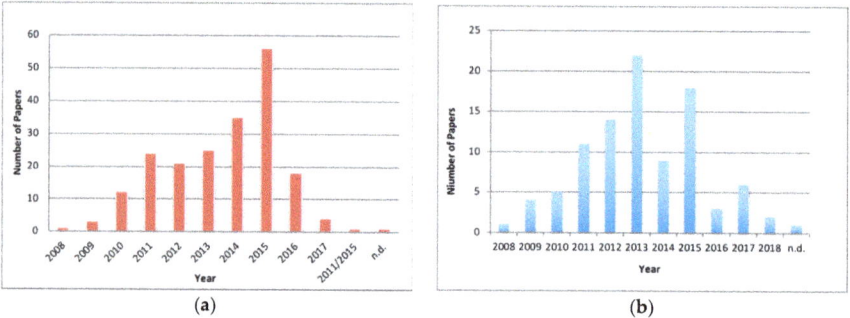

(a)   (b)

Figure 3. Number of publications referencing the (a) FRAME model and (b) 3-LEF, by publication date.

6.2. Types of Publications

The majority of the papers were published in journals followed by conference papers (Table 5). Both the 3-LEF and FRAME model were also mentioned in a significant number of dissertations and master's theses.

Table 5. Publication types.

Publication Type	FRAME		3-LEF	
	All *	Applied **	All *	Applied **
Blog	1	1	0	0
Book	5	1	0	0
Book chapter	10	0	11	0
Conference paper	46	15	19	5
Conference poster	1	1	0	0
Doctoral dissertation	41	8	4	0
Journal article	87	24	57	2
Master's thesis	5	2	5	3
Report	7	3	0	0
Unknown type	2	0	1	0
Wiki entry	1	0	0	0
Total	208	55	97	10

* Note: "All" includes all publications regardless of whether or not the model/framework was applied in research.
** Note: "Applied' includes only publications in which the model/framework was applied to conduct research.

6.3. Geographic Reach

Our team was interested in geographic reach; that is, to what extent researchers in other countries are aware of the 3-LEF and the FRAME model. For each paper, we considered the location of each author (i.e., where s/he works) and, if indicated, the country in which the research was conducted. Table 6 shows the number of countries (authors' location and country of research) for all publications and the number of countries (authors' location and country of research) for those publications in which the FRAME or 3-LEF was applied.

Table 6. Number of countries.

Country of	FRAME (All Publications)	FRAME (Applied Only)	3-LEF (All Publications)	3-LEF (Applied Only)
Author	45	26	38	4
Research	39	22	26	5

6.4. Areas of Research

The 3-LEF and the FRAME model were referenced within publications belonging to a variety of fields and contexts. During this project, our team documented whenever the authors of the papers indicated areas of their research. We collapsed the areas into five major categories:

- Education levels;
- School subjects;
- Learning activities and skills development;
- Uptake, support, design of mobile systems; and
- Issues, challenges, and potentials of mobile learning.

Appendix B lists the areas of research within the five categories. It appears that the greatest number of studies were in the area of higher education. Within the learning activities category, gamification, contextual learning, field trips, and the use of social networks are the greatest in number. There was a wide variety of school subject areas across all the publications, but language learning and health-related subjects were very strongly represented. In the uptake, design, and support category, studies of learner uptake, attitudes, and support were most numerous, followed by the design and evaluation of learning environments and studies of pedagogical practices.

6.5. Research Methods and Methodologies

Table 7 lists the methods and methodologies using the nomenclature of the original authors for all studies and only those that applied the FRAME model and 3-LEF in their research.

Table 7. Methods and methodologies as named by the authors.

Method/Methodology	FRAME	FRAME Applied	3-LEF	3-LEF Applied
Action research	2	1	0	0
Actor Network Theory	1	0	0	0
Artifact collection	1	0	0	0
Case study	19	6	8	2
Content analysis	1	1	0	0
Conversation analysis	0	0	1	0
Cooperative inquiry	0	0	1	0
Delphi study	1	0	2	0
Descriptive study	1	1	0	0
Design-based research	2	0	2	0
Diary	0	0	2	0
Ethnography	1	1	0	0

Table 7. *Cont.*

Method/Methodology	FRAME	FRAME Applied	3-LEF	3-LEF Applied
Experimental/quasi-experimental	10	5	8	3
Explanatory study	1	1	1	0
Exploratory study	1	0	0	0
Evaluation study	5	3	7	3
Focus groups	5	2	3	1
Grounded theory	1	0	0	0
Interaction analysis	0	0	1	0
Interviews	9	1	5	2
Mixed methods	15	4	13	5
Observation	0	0	3	0
Phenomenography	1	1	0	0
Phenomenology	2	0	0	0
Survey/questionnaire	24	8	7	4
Systematic review	20	0	13	0
Task analysis	0	0	1	0
Testing knowledge	2	0	0	0
Visual methodology	1	0	0	0

6.6. Contributions of the Seminal Articles

As our research team read through the publications that cited the 3-LEF, we began to note some patterns in how the seminal articles were being referenced. As such, it became clear that the works that initially introduced the FRAME model and 3-LEF contributed to the field in more general ways—that is, outside of evaluation and conceptual work. In the following section, the numbers in the tables offer a sense of proportion of the topics mentioned.

6.6.1. FRAME Model Comments in the Literature

Out of 65 references (outside of papers that explicitly used the model in their research), 42 publications made minor references to the FRAME model. Of those that more explicitly cited the two seminal articles [4,5], Table 8 summarizes the topics that were the most mentioned.

Table 8. Most referenced topics (*n* = 65).

Topic *	References
Anytime anywhere access	5
Cognitive issues (especially load)	7
Context	6
Convergence of aspects (device, learner, social)	41
Definition of mobile learning	3
Knowledge navigation	6
Minor mention **	42
Social emphasis of the model	14
Technological limitations & characteristics	18
Utility in designing learning tools and practices	8

* Note: Some articles mentioned more than one topic. ** Minor mentions refer to those that mention the model/framework and/or seminal articles in non-substantial ways; a "nod" of acknowledgement.

We observed that many authors were attracted by the notion that mobile learning comprises multiple aspects. At the same time, some authors focused their research on a particular aspect such as the social. Others made explicit reference to technological characteristics of mobile devices.

6.6.2. 3-LEF Comments in the Literature

We coded 59 instances of authors citing the two seminal articles on the 3-LEF [6,7]. Of these, we coded 35 comments as minor mentions. Table 9 summarizes the topics that were the most mentioned.

Table 9. Most referenced topics (*n* = 59).

Topic *	3-LEF
Challenges in evaluation	8
Definition clarification	4
Evaluation methods	5
Examples of evaluation studies	12
In/formal learning and context	9
Micro, meso, macro levels	6
Minor mentions **	35
The need for evaluation studies	11
Mobile as social rather than technological	4

* Note: Some articles mentioned more than one topic. ** Minor mentions refer to those that mention the model/framework and/or seminal articles in non-substantial ways; a "nod" of acknowledgement.

Vavoula and Sharples' work was very often mentioned in a list of examples of evaluation (12 instances) studies in mobile learning. There were 11 instances where researchers explicitly argued for additional evaluation studies. There were four incidents in which the authors referred to the 3-LEF articles in order to clarify definitions such as mobile learning, location-based learning, and microsites. Six authors explicitly mentioned the micro, meso, and macro perspectives. Authors also drew upon the 3-LEF publications to champion the view that mobile learning is primarily a social rather than a technological phenomenon.

6.7. Reasons for Use

Our team searched for statements that explicitly stated why the researchers chose to use the model/framework to conduct their research.

6.7.1. Reasons for Using the FRAME Model

Seven of the eleven references coded for "reasons for use" indicated that the main appeal of the FRAME model is that is gives equal footing to the learner, the social and the technological aspects of mobile learning [25,26]. One author suggested that the model not only outlines the relationship between the three aspects but also addresses contemporary pedagogical issues of information overload, knowledge navigation, and collaborative learning [27]. Another work found that the choice of what to evaluate was alleviated, as all three aspects are equally important and should, therefore, all be evaluated [28]. Sandpearl [29] comments that maximum learning potential is achieved when the interactions between the social, the device, and learner converge.

Some authors showed interest in the social aspects of mobile learning [30]. Others commented that the FRAME model supports a socio-cultural view of learning [31,32]. Others appreciated the constructivist approach underlying the model and that it is an appropriate tool for examining learning and collaboration [25,26].

Several authors stated that the FRAME model was intuitive and easier to use than other models [26,33]. The accompanying checklist of key items and questions to guide the development of mobile learning applications [5] appears to have contributed to the perceived ease of use [24,34,35].

6.7.2. Reasons for Using the 3-LEF Framework

Three publications provided some insight into why they used the 3-LEF. One suggested that the framework, with the embedded micro, meso, and macro levels, acknowledges the ambiguity in the relationship between learning and the role of the institution [36]. The second indicated that the ability to evaluate at all stages along the development trajectory was key in the choice to adopt the 3-LEF [37]. And, the third paper indicated that the 3-LEF was selected because there were no other models specifically designed for wearable technology (a head-mounted display) [38].

6.8. Critiques of Model/Framework

Critiques of the model/framework were much easier to locate than rationales for their use. Our analysis revealed some astute observations and as well as some misconceptions of the models and the field of mobile learning overall. Although expressing appreciation for the 3-LEF and the FRAME model, some authors suggested that there is a lack of frameworks and models and, of the existing models, none of them are sufficient for guiding the design of mobile learning in varying contexts [35,39].

There were many critiques of mobile learning models in general. In these cases, the FRAME model and/or the 3-LEF were listed amongst other models:

- They have a limited perspective on context as they do not include the role of media at producing learning contexts. No methodologies or tools are available yet that treat the virtualization of context in an explicit way [40].
- They are limited in their practical applicability because they have no defined guidelines that consider the stages for the deployment of m-learning, but they do serve as starting points for the development of a sustainable M-learning model [41]. As such, there is need to bridge the gap between pre- and post-implementation phases in order to ensure sustainability.
- Do not address the question of how best to implement mobile learning in formal education [42].
- These frameworks are not learning theories per se. Rather, they offer ways to evaluate and frame mobile learning activities within the ubiquitous landscape of mobile learning [43]. It was also noted that the models lacked investigation into some macro-level factors including cultural and social barriers. Therefore, some papers highlighted the need for consideration and integration of broader social contexts when examining the efficacy of specific mobile learning contexts and research [44].

6.8.1. Critiques of the FRAME Model

Critiques specifically focusing on the FRAME model referred to missing criteria. Observing that the FRAME model defines mobile learning in terms of the interactions between learners, their devices, and other people [45], Wishart, cautions that Koole's conceptual model does not acknowledge the potential mobility of the learner whose technology enables them to use information and data from one context to another. Khaddage et al. state that the FRAME model fails to address factors such as policies, pedagogy, technology, and innovative research in the field [46]; therefore, more guidance about how to utilize emerging mobile technologies and integrate them seamlessly into teaching and learning is still needed [46].

Power proposed an instructional-design related model that explicitly guides pedagogical issues [47]. He posited that although the FRAME model presents a holistic picture of the domains to be considered when designing or redesigning mobile learning initiatives, it does not provide guidance on the pedagogical design considerations needed for creating an effective collaborative learning experience for the learner [47].

Some critiques were more general in nature. For example, one paper argued that the FRAME model is a conceptual proposal and, hence, does not explore whether it would be suitable in real scenarios for supporting the development and adoption of its approaches [18]. Another researcher stated that the FRAME model is not yet sufficient given that further understanding of the highly dynamic emerging field of mobile learning is required [49]. Other authors indicated that Koole's

FRAME model is not applicable in primary education because it was "constructed in a higher education context, [which is] quite different from that of primary education" [50].

6.8.2. Critiques of the 3-LEF Model

We coded 11 instances of "critique" amongst the 97 publications. Some authors suggest that there is a general lack of systematic evaluation studies in the field of mobile learning. One paper includes a discussion of the 3-LEF but subsequently claims that the field of mobile learning lacks evaluation models/frameworks that have been "systematically and rigorously applied and fleshed out" [39]. Having listed a number of studies "conceptualizing" mobile learning, one paper indicated that no prior publications had adequately or rigorously measured success, scalability, and replicability of mobile learning initiatives. However, the author(s) offer no specific critiques of the 3-LEF (or other frameworks) were offered [51].

Farley and Murphy suggest that the 3-LEF was overly focused on the social characteristics of mobile learning to the detriment of the technical [39]. Another author praises the 3-LEF for its complex gap analysis and design heuristics but rejects the framework because it does not provide evaluation criteria [52].

Finally, we found an interesting critique of the micro-meso-macro approach: that it would require researchers to switch perspectives during the research project [53]. The authors suggested that perspective switching could result in communication issues and confusion because people working at one level would lack understanding of the impact [of the mobile intervention] on those working at other levels.

6.9. Extensions and Modifications

Our review of the literature revealed that some researchers suggested modifications to the FRAME model and the 3-LEF. Our team also noticed instances in which the FRAME and the 3-LEF were blended with other models.

6.9.1. Modifications to the FRAME Model

Some authors claim to have extended the FRAME model. For example, Norman, Din, and Nordin altered the model so that it would be based on four aspects: web 3.0 technology, learner context-awareness, learner cognition, and learner social skills [54]. Boyinbode, Ng'ambi, and Bagula integrated Anderson's six types of educational interactions, something that they thought had not been addressed directly in the original FRAME model [55]. Meanwhile, Levene and Seabury combined the FRAME model with Park's transactional distance theory model in an effort to inform instructional design practices [56].

The relational structure of the FRAME model was also modified. For example, the "augmented FRAME" was designed in order to differentiate K-2 learning methods based on characteristics such as targeted grade level, specific devices, necessary infrastructure, mobility, cost per student, and type of learning [50]. Pani and Mishra offer a modified view in which there are four aspects (social, learner, device, and context) and four intersections (device usability, interaction learning, mobility interaction, and pervasiveness) [57]. Finally, Wong recommended a new mobile learning model where he has embedded a curriculum aspect into the Koole's FRAME model and places the learner aspect into the center of the FRAME model [27]. He suggests that the curriculum aspect should be evaluated in future research studies to find out how mobile informal learning experiences or activities can assist students in formal learning contexts.

Some authors offered less extensive modifications such as the addition of "mobile pedagogy" considerations that complement the socio-cultural characteristics of the FRAME model [32]. Another author suggested that instead of mobile learning, ubiquitous learning or pervasive learning could occupy the center of the Venn diagram [57]. Lefrere also recommended that the FRAME model include networking and networked services. In this way, researchers would acknowledge the surface functionality of a device as well as the functionality it gains through networking [58].

6.9.2. Modifications to the 3-LEF

There was no evidence of major modifications proposed for the 3-LEF. We documented only one minor modification. In one study, the author(s) examined the micro and meso levels in depth [53]. At the micro level, they added a mobile quality piece to the evaluation.

Our Nvivo code "extends other model" captured some evidence that elements of the 3-LEF were used to enhance other evaluation models/frameworks. In one dissertation, the author combined the 3-LEF with other models in order to create his/her own evaluation criteria [59]. Another study focused on the meso level (learner experience) whilst proposing a new model developed in order to highlight socio-cultural characteristics of mobile learning [32].

7. Discussion

7.1. Number of References

As mentioned, at the time of writing, Google Scholar indicated that the FRAME model had been referenced over 500 times and the 3-LEF over 200 times. Our team searched eight databases for any publications referencing the seminal articles that introduced the models [4–7]. Our team removed from analysis articles that referenced the seminal articles without actually discussing or citing them in their body text. Our final analysis was left with 208 articles citing the FRAME model and 97 for the 3-LEF.

One of our main goals was to explore the impact that the FRAME model and the 3-LEF have had in educational research. A preliminary look at numeric data in reference indices suggests that both models are well represented in conference presentations and journal articles. Surprisingly, the FRAME model has been mentioned in an unusually high number of doctoral dissertations (see Table 5). Overall, the FRAME model appears to have been more referenced than the 3-LEF. This might be due to the more general, conceptual nature of the FRAME model. It might also be related to the publication of the 2009 article [5] in a free, open-access publication.

7.2. Reasons for Use

As alluded to earlier, the both models were applied in ways that were not originally predicted by the Koole, Vavoula, and Sharples (summarized in Table 2). Although originally designed for qualitative analysis, the FRAME model has been used in quantitative studies in which researchers have attempted to develop numeric measures of mobile characteristics [60,61]. In the case of the 3-LEF, some researchers chose to implement it at only one level of granularity such as the micro or the meso [62,63]. Both of these examples suggest healthy innovation.

Although there were a number of topics that were mentioned in the literature, our team took special note that both the FRAME and the 3-LEF were recognized for emphasizing the social characteristics of learning (See Tables 8 and 9). We would argue that both models, while having strongly supporting a social view of learning, also place significance on other factors within the mobile learning milieu. To a greater or lesser extent, they both involve examining the physical environment and technology.

Both models recognized the interrelationship of multiple components that are often treated separately in research such as

- The social, learner, and technical aspects;
- The micro, meso, and macro levels;
- The phases of development; and
- The stages of evaluation.

In our analysis, we gained a sense that the multi-components approach was a drawing feature of both the FRAME and the 3-LEF.

7.3. Critiques

Naturally, critiques were often used by authors in order to argue in favour of a new model they were proposing. Models such as the FRAME and 3-LEF were viewed by some as a starting point, but that they were lacking in some ways. Some authors appeared to require evaluation criteria or guidelines that were customized to their study contexts and phenomena such as virtualization of context, in/formal learning situations, and ubiquitous landscapes. Similarly, one paper suggested that neither model allowed for use in formal education settings. However, both the FRAME and the 3-LEF are deliberately designed to accommodate a wide variety of contexts and phenomena. And, the authors of both the FRAME model and the 3-LEF have acknowledged their applicability beyond mobile learning. As one writer correctly observed, they are conceptual/evaluative tools [44]. As such, they were designed with some flexibility and openness permitting customization for specific contexts and phenomena.

The critique that the FRAME and the 3-LEF (1) do not include the role of media in producing learning contexts [40] and (2) that factors such as cultural and social barriers are not considered lacks consistency with our reading of the FRAME model and the 3-LEF. The role of media and social barriers fit neatly within the models. For example, media can be represented in the technology aspect of the FRAME model (see Figure 1) and is embedded throughout the design processes in the 3-LEF (see Figure 2). Furthermore, social barriers can be discussed within the social aspect and the social-interaction intersection of the FRAME model. The 3-LEF was developed within a socio-cultural perspective; therefore, social issues can be examined through the ongoing interviews with users embedded within the evaluation process.

Interestingly, another critique of the 3-LEF was that it is overly focused on the social to the detriment of the technical [50]. If the scope of a research project is to examine only the technological aspects of a mobile learning initiative, then it is logical that the researcher would modify it so as to focus on a particular characteristic.

Finally, there was a criticism that neither model is a learning theory per se. That is true, these models were not designed as learning theories. One would choose to use the FRAME model to gain a conceptual understanding of a mobile learning situation or to guide the design of a mobile learning application. One would use the 3-LEF to evaluate a mobile learning situation or application. Nonetheless, both models were conceptualized and developed within perspectives such as social constructivism, situated-learning, and socio-cultural theories. As we have discovered through this research, both have been applied in the design of learning applications. Therefore, we argue that models can be used creatively and flexibly.

7.4. Modifications

The information context in the FRAME model is often overlooked (See Figure 1). The information context asks researchers to define the scope; all aspects and intersections fit within each, defined context. The authors of the "augmented FRAME" did not so much create a new version of the model but changed the scope appropriately. Rejecting the model for contextual reasons, requires careful thought. For example, suggesting that it cannot be applied to a K-12 context can be contested. Although the FRAME model was originally developed within a higher education context, the original Master's thesis by Koole [4] includes learning theories that connect various levels of education. Koole, for example, refers to Vygotsky's zone of proximal development [15], which is most often associated with childhood learning processes. Furthermore, if the context is K-12 or in/formal learning, it can be defined in the information context. The characteristics of all the aspects would be described within the specified context. More thought should also be given to the addition of an extra circle for context [57]; because the context is already a part of the FRAME model, the extra circle seems redundant.

As educators, we strive to ensure that learners occupy a significant place in education. Wong reconfigured the FRAME model so as to place the learner at the center of the mobile learning process. However, this upsets logic of set theory. When circles overlap, there are shared elements. The overlapping of all the circles cannot result in a learner aspect; the center must contain element of all the circles. In addition, in the original FRAME model, the curriculum is part of the social learning intersection (See Figure 1). Currently, as Koole moves toward a more socio-materialist philosophy, the co-creation of the social and the material is jeopardized when the human is positioned as more significant than the other elements [22]. Wong's work, however, is highly valuable. In future descriptions of the social-learning intersection, curriculum should be explicitly listed. Similarly, Pani and Mishra's work has led us to consider whether the social-learning intersection could be more aptly named "mobile pedagogy" [57].

Lefrere's suggestion that ubiquitous or pervasive learning could occupy the center of the FRAME model (see Figure 1) is an astute observation [58]. This suggests that there is some thinking about how the model(s) can be successfully transitioned to different technologies. However, it is unclear if Lefrere is suggesting that mobile learning and ubiquitous or pervasive learning are the same phenomenon. And, this brings us to questions of definitions and nomenclature. There may be a philosophical piece here that requires further deliberation. Does the different nomenclature suggest a shift in semantics surrounding mobile learning or a shift in the ontology of mobile learning?

8. Conclusions and Future Research

This paper has only examined two of many models in the field of mobile learning. The FRAME and the 3-LEF models were selected for this study because they have amassed more than 10 years of references. It is encouraging that the models have been implemented across a wide range of topics, fields of study, and geographic contexts. As researchers and practitioners, our team had hoped to gain some insights into how researchers selected and rejected models/frameworks. The critiques, reasons for use, and modifications have provided us with additional ideas of how we might "tweak" the FRAME and 3-LEF in our own work.

At a more general level, we have begun thinking about how researchers in the mobile learning field are approaching model selection and evaluation. While some authors indicated that they were drawn to the constructivist approach of the FRAME model (Koole's original approach) and the socio-cultural emphasis of both the FRAME and the 3-LEF, there was little evidence for conscious selection of models/frameworks based on ontological or epistemological concerns. We are left with some perplexing questions: Are mobile learning specialists making logistical decisions in which models/frameworks are chosen for criteria such as ease of use? Are they basing their decisions on a particular philosophical position, or are we seeing the emergence of new models because there is something yet unforeseen, and therefore unaddressed, in the nature of mobile learning? Similar reviews of other models would help us understand how mobile learning researchers and practitioners evaluate and choose their research tools.

Author Contributions: Conceptualization, M.K.; Data curation, R.B., K.A. and D.L.; Formal analysis, M.K.; Methodology, M.K.; Project administration, M.K.; Writing—original draft, M.K.; Writing—review & editing, M.K., R.B., K.A. and D.L.

funding: This research was funded by the Office of the Provost Faculty Recruitment and Retention Program, University of Saskatchewan grant number 416033.

Acknowledgments: Special thanks to John Traxler who suggested we examine two models/frameworks in tandem.

Appendix A

Table A1. Nvivo codes and descriptions.

Top Level Node	Sub Node	Description
Applied		The model/framework was applied.
Area		Field or area of the paper (i.e., museums, biology, architecture, etc.).
Conclusions		Significant conclusion or results from research.
Country of author		Country in which the author lives/works.
Country of research		Country in which the research was conducted.
Critique		Critiques of the FRAME or 3-LEF.
Date		Year of publication.
Extends another model		The seminal paper, model/framework was used to develop or extend a different model.
Literature review		The seminal paper, model/framework was mentioned in the literature (or other parts of the paper).
Methods/methodology		These nodes are used to document the types of papers or studies as described by the authors themselves. Most names are self-explanatory.
	Action research	
	ANT	Actor Network Theory.
	Content analysis	
	Conversation analysis	
	Delphi study	
	Diary	Journal, notes.
	Ethnography	
	Focus groups	
	Grounded theory	
	Interaction analysis	
	Interviews	
	Observation	Qualitative or quantitative uses.
	Phenomenography	
	Phenomenology	
	Survey	Includes questionnaires; qualitative or quantitative.
	Task analysis	
	Visual methodology	
	Experimental	Quantitative.
	Quasi-experimental	Quantitative.
	Testing knowledge	Quantitative.
	Artifact collection	
	Case study	
	Descriptive study	
	Design-based research	
	Explanatory study	
	Exploratory study	
	Systematic review	Document review, extensive literature review.
	Evaluation study	
	Qualitative	Author indicated qualitative but did not specify.
	Quantitative	Author indicated quantitative but did not specify.
	Mixed methods	Author indicated mixed methods but did not specify.
Publication type		
	Blog	
	Book	
	Book chapter	
	Conference paper	
	Conference poster	
	Doctoral dissertation/thesis	
	Journal article	
	Master's thesis	
	Report	
	Unknown	
	Wiki entry	
Reason for use		The author explicitly states why s/he chose the FRAME or the 3-LEF.
Reference only		The seminal paper is referenced, but not mentioned or cited in the paper.
Springboard to new ideas		The model/framework was used to develop a completely new model/framework.

Appendix B

Table A2. Areas of research in which the FRAME and 3-LEF were cited.

Areas of Research *	3-LEF 97 References	3-LEF Applied 10 References	FRAME 201 References	FRAME Applied 81 References
Education levels				
Basic, elementary childhood	4	0	7	3
High school	1	1	0	0
Higher education (college, university)	4	0	19	7
Informal, non-formal (any age)	2	1	3	1
Lifelong learning (adults)	0	0	2	0
Middle school	0	0	2	1
Total	11	2	33	12
School subjects				
Architecture	0	0	2	1
Art	0	0	2	1
Biology	1	1	0	0
Business	1	0	2	1
Computer science	1	0	2	0
Construction training	1	0	0	0
Corporate training (incl. banking)	1	0	1	1
Drama	0	0	1	1
Engineering	0	0	1	0
Health (nursing, medicine, first aid)	1	0	11	4
Language learning	2	0	20	5
Marine education	0	0	1	1
Mathematics	2	2	1	0
Natural resources	0	0	1	0
Nature	1	0	1	0
Religion	0	0	1	0
Robotics	1	0	0	0
Sport	0	0	2	2
STEM/STEAM	0	0	1	0
Travel and tourism	1	0	1	0
Total	13	3	51	17
Learning activities and skills development				
Collaborative learning	1	0	2	1
Contextual (ambient) learning	4	0	3	0
Field trips (including museums)	4	0	1	1
Gamification of learning	3	1	5	2
Intercultural competence	1	0	0	0
Literacy, computer, numeracy	1	0	4	0
Metacognitive skills	2	0	0	0
MOOC	0	0	1	0
Social networks	2	0	6	2
Virtual reality	1	0	0	0
Wearable technology	1	1	0	0
Total	20	2	22	6
Uptake, design, and support				
Disabled learner support	0	0	4	2
Evaluation	5	2	0	0
Faculty uptake, support, and attitudes	0	0	9	1
Institutional uptake, attitudes, support, policy	1	1	3	1
Instructional/learning design	3	0	11	4
Learner uptake, attitudes, and support	7	2	19	4
Learning environments–design, evaluation	7	0	16	9
Pedagogical practices	6	0	14	4
Teacher (K-12) training, attitudes, and support	3	0	10	3
Total	32	5	86	28
M-Learning issues, challenges, potentials				
Access to education	2	0	3	1
Developing world	0	0	6	1
Distance education	0	0	3	0
M-learning issues, challenges, and benefits	11	1	20	1
Theories, models, frameworks	3	1	10	1
Total	16	2	42	4

* Note: The overall totals do not add up to the total number of studies because some studies indicated more than one area/topic.

References

1. Crompton, H. A Historical overview of m-learning: Toward learner-centred education. In *Handbook of Mobile Learning*; Berge, Z.L., Muilenburg, L.Y., Eds.; Taylor & Francis Ltd.: New York, NY, USA, 2013; pp. 3–14.
2. Miles, M.; Huberman, A. *Qualitative Data Analysis: An Expanded Source Book*, 2nd ed.; Sage Publications: Thousand Oaks, CA, USA, 1994.
3. Harvey, J. (Ed.) *Evaluation Cookbook*; Heriot-Watt University: Edinburgh, UK, 1998.
4. Koole, M. The Framework for the Rational Analysis of Mobile Education (Frame) Model: An Evaluation of Mobile Devices for Distance Education. Master's Thesis, Athabasca University, Athabasca, AB, Canada, 2006.
5. Koole, M. A model for framing mobile learning. In *Mobile Learning: Transforming the Delivery of Education and Training*; Ally, M., Ed.; Issues in Distance Education; AU Press: Edmonton, AB, Canada, 2009; Volume 1, pp. 25–47.
6. Vavoula, G.; Sharples, M. Meeting the challenges in evaluating mobile learning: A 3-level evaluation framework. *Int. J. Mob. Blended Learn.* **2009**, *1*, 54–75. [CrossRef]
7. Vavoula, G.; Sharples, M.; Rudman, P.; Meek, J.; Lonsdale, P. Myartspace: Design and evaluation of support for learning with multimedia phones between classrooms and museums. *Comput. Educ.* **2009**, *53*, 286–299. [CrossRef]
8. Yanchar, S.C.; Gibbons, A.S.; Gabbitas, B.W.; Matthews, M.T. Critical thinking in the field of educational technology: Approaches, projects, and challenges. In *Educational Media and Technology Yearbook*; Orey, M., McClendon, V.J., Branch, R.M., Eds.; Springer: Chan, Switzerland, 2017; pp. 127–147.
9. Danziger, K. The methodological imperative in psychology. *Philos. Soc. Sci. Des. Sci.* **1985**, *15*, 1–13. [CrossRef]
10. Ally, M. *Mobile Learning: Transforming the Delivery of Education and Training*; Anderson, T., Ed.; AU Press: Edmonton, AB, Canada, 2009.
11. Ausubel, D.P. *Educational Psychology: A Cognitive View*; Rinehart and Winston, Inc.: New York, NY, USA, 1968.
12. Bruner, J. *The Process of Education: A Searching Discussion of School Education Opening New Paths to Learning and Teaching*; Vintage Books: New York, NY, USA, 1960.
13. Gagné, R.M. *The Conditions of Learning*; Holt, Rinehart and Winston, Inc.: New York, NY, USA, 1977.
14. Paivio, A. *Imagery and Verbal Processing*; Holt, Rinehart and Winston, Inc.: New York, NY, USA, 1971.
15. Vygotsky, L.S. *Mind in Society: The Development of Higher Psychological Processes*; Harvard University Press: Cambridge, MA, USA, 1978.
16. Wenger, E. *Communities of Practice: Learning, Meaning, and Identity*; Cambridge University Press: Edinburgh, UK, 1998.
17. Nielsen, J. *Usability Engineering*; Academic Press: London, UK, 1994.
18. Preece, J.; Rogers, Y.; Sharp, H. *Interaction Design: Beyond Human-Computer Interaction*, 2nd ed.; Wiley Publishing, Inc.: Hoboken, NJ, USA, 2002.
19. Shneiderman, B.; Plaisant, C. *Designing the User Interface: Strategies for Effective Human-Computer Interaction*, 4th ed.; Pearson Education Inc.: Toronto, ON, Canada, 2004.
20. Moore, M.G. Editorial: Three types of interaction. *Am. J. Distance Educ.* **1989**, *3*, 1–6. [CrossRef]
21. Keegan, D. *Foundations of Distance Education*; Routledge: London, UK, 1996; Volume 3.
22. Koole, M.L. Mobile learning, teacher education, and the sociomaterialist perspective: Analysis of the SMS story project. *Int. J. Mob. Blended Learn.* **2018**, *10*, 66–77. [CrossRef]
23. Meek, J. Adopting a Lifecycle Approach to the Evaluation of Computer and Information Technology. Ph.D. Thesis, University of Birmingham, Birmingham, UK, 2006.
24. Hsu, Y.-C.; Ching, Y.-H. A review of models and frameworks for designing mobile learning experiences and environments. *Can. J. Learn. Technol.* **2015**, *41*. [CrossRef]
25. Hansson, P.-O.; Jobe, W. Smart Running in Kenya Kenyan Runners' Improvement in Training, Informal Learning and Economic Opportunities Using Smartphones. In Proceedings of the IST-Africa 2013 Conference & Exhibition, Nairobi, Kenya, 29–31 May 2013.
26. Hosler, K.A. Pedagogies, Perspectives, and Practices: Mobile Learning through the Experiences of Faculty Developers and Instructional Designers in Centers for Teaching and Learning. Ph.D. Thesis, University of Northern Colorado, Greeley, CO, USA, 2013.

27. Wong, C.H.H. A Study of Mobile Learning for Guangzhou's University Students. Ph.D. Thesis, Guangzhou University, Guangzhou, China, 2015.

28. Levene, J.; Seabury, H. Evaluation of mobile learning: Current research and implications for instructional designers. *TechTrends* **2015**, *59*, 46–52. [CrossRef]

29. Sandpearl, H. Digital Apps and Learning in a Senior Theatre Class. Master's Thesis, University of Melbourne, Melbourne, Austrlia, 2016.

30. Cheung, R. Predicting user intentions for mobile learning in a project-based environment. *Int. J. Electron. Commer. Stud.* **2013**, *4*, 263. [CrossRef]

31. Kearney, M.; Burden, K.; Rai, T. Investigating teachers' adoption of signature mobile pedagogies. *Comput. Educ.* **2015**, *80*, 48–57. [CrossRef]

32. Kearney, M.; Schuck, S.; Burden, K.; Aubusson, P. Viewing mobile learning from a pedagogical perspective. *Res. Learn. Technol.* **2012**, *20*, 1–17. [CrossRef]

33. Bird, T. Places: Evaluating Mobile Learning. Available online: https://placesmobile.wordpress.com/ (accessed on 30 April 2018).

34. Haag, J.; Berking, P. Design considerations for mobile learning. In *Handbook of Mobile Teaching and Learning*; Springer: Berlin, Germany, 2015; pp. 41–60.

35. Hsu, Y.-C.; Ching, Y.-H.; Snelson, C. Research priorities in mobile learning: An international Delphi study. *Can. J. Learn. Technol.* **2014**, *40*. [CrossRef]

36. Bryant, P.; Coombs, A.; Pazio, M.; Walker, S. Disruption, Destruction, Construction or Transformation? The Challenges of Implementing a University Wide Strategic Approach to Connecting in an Open World. In Proceedings of the 2014 OCW Consortium Global Conference: Open Education for a Multicultural World, Ljubljana, Slovenia, 23–25 April 2014; pp. 23–25.

37. Timoko, T. Towards an Indigenous Model for Effective Mobile Learning. In Proceedings of the International Conference on Mobile and Contextual Learning, Istanbul, Turkey, 3–5 November 2014; pp. 315–320.

38. Du, X. Design and Evaluation of a Learning Assistant System with Optical Head-Mounted Display (OHMD). Master's Thesis, Carleton University, Ottawa, ON, Canada, 2014.

39. Farley, H.; Murphy, A. Developing a framework for evaluating the impact and sustainability of mobile learning initiatives in higher education. In Proceedings of the Open and Distance Learning Association of Australia Distance Education Summit (ODLAA 2013), Sydney, Australia, 4–6 February 2013; pp. 27–34.

40. Westera, W. On the changing nature of learning context: Anticipating the virtual extensions of the world. *J. Educ. Technol. Soc.* **2011**, *14*, 201–212.

41. Abu-Al-Aish, A. Toward Mobile Learning Deployment in Higher Education. Ph.D. Thesis, Brunel University, London, UK, 2014.

42. Lawson, R.; Snow, K. *Turn on Your Phones Please: From Distaction to Engagement with Mobile Learning*; The Association of Atlantic Universities and Cape Breton University: Halifax, NS, Canada, 2015; Volume 18.

43. McCallum, K.; Parsons, D. A Theory-Ology of Mobile Learning: Operationalizing Learning Theories with Mobile Activities. In *Mobile Learning Futures—Sustaining Quality Research and Practice in Mobile Learning (mLearn), Proceedings of the 15th World Conference on Mobile and Contextual Learning, Sydney, Australia, 24–26 October 2016*; Dyson, L.E., Wan, N., Fergusson, J., Eds.; Unitec Research Bank: Sydney, Australia, 2016; pp. 173–182.

44. Wei, Y.; So, H.-J. Three-level evaluation framework for a systematic review of contextual mobile learning. In Proceedings of the 11th International Conference on Mobile and Contextual Learning, Helsinki, Finland, 16–18 October 2012; pp. 164–171.

45. Wishart, J. *Assimilate or Accommodate? The Need to Rethink Current Use of the Term 'Mobile Learning'*; The Mobile Learning Voyage-From Small Ripples to Massive Open Waters; Springer: Berlin, Germany, 2015; pp. 229–238.

46. Khaddage, F.; Christensen, R.; Lai, W.; Knezek, G.; Norris, C.; Soloway, E. A model driven framework to address challenges in a mobile learning environment. *Educ. Inf. Technol.* **2015**, *20*, 625–640. [CrossRef]

47. Power, R. A Framework for Promoting Teacher Self-Efficacy with Mobile Reusable Learning Objects. Ph.D. Thesis, Athabasca University, Athabasca, AB, Canada, 2015.

48. Alvarez, C.; Alarcon, R.; Nussbaum, M. Implementing collaborative learning activities in the classroom supported by one-to-one mobile computing: A design-based process. *J. Syst. Softw.* **2011**, *84*, 1961–1976. [CrossRef]

49. Crompton, H. A theory of mobile learning. In *International Handbook of E-Learning Volume 1 Theoretical Perspectives and Research*; Routledge: London, UK, 2015; Volume 2, p. 309.

50. Bachman, K.M.; Gannod, G.C. A Critical Analysis of M-Learning Initiatives. In *Mobile Learning 2011*; Sanchez, I.A., Isaias, P., Eds.; International Association for Development of the Information Society: Avila, Spain, 2011; p. 310.

51. Alrasheedi, M.; Capretz, L.F. Applying CMM towards an m-learning context. In *Information Society (i-Society)*; Infonomics Society: Essex, UK, 2013.

52. Harpur, P.-A.; de Villiers, R. MUUX-E, a framework of criteria for evaluating the usability, user experience and educational features of m-learning environments. *S. Afr. Comput. J.* **2015**, *56*, 1–21. [CrossRef]

53. McAndrew, P.; Taylor, J.; Clow, D. Facing the challenge in evaluating technology use in mobile environments. *J. Open Distance E-Learn.* **2010**, *25*, 233–249. [CrossRef]

54. Norman, H.; Din, R.; Nordin, N. A preliminary study of an authentic ubiquitous learning environment for higher education. In Proceedings of the 10th WSEAS International Conference on E-Activities, Jakarta, Indonesia, 1–3 December 2011; Volume 3, pp. 5–6.

55. Boyinbode, O.; Ng'ambi, D. MOBILect: An interactive mobile lecturing tool for fostering deep learning. *Int. J. Mob. Learn. Organ.* **2015**, *9*, 182–200. [CrossRef]

56. Park, Y. A pedagogical framework for mobile learning: Categorizing educational applications of mobile technologies into four types. *Int. Rev. Res. Open Distrib. Learn.* **2011**, *12*, 78–102. [CrossRef]

57. Pani, S.; Mishra, J. An effective mobile learning model for learning through mobile apps. *IBMRD's J. Manag. Res.* **2015**, *4*, 20–37. [CrossRef]

58. Lefrere, P. Activity-based scenarios for approaches to ubiquitous e-learning. *Pers. Ubiquitous Comput.* **2009**, *13*, 219–227. [CrossRef]

59. Harpur, P.-A. Evaluation of Usability and User Experience of an M-Learning Environment, Custom-Designed for a Tertiary Educational Context. Ph.D. Thesis, University of South Africa, Pretoria, South Africa, 2013.

60. Fulbright, R. A Quantitative Study Investigating the Effect of Motivational Text Messages in Online Learning. Ph.D. Thesis, Northcentral University, Scottsdale, AZ, USA, 2012.

61. Talebi, F.; Sasaniyan, M. A study on the FRAME model: Evidence from the banking industry. *Manag. Sci. Lett.* **2015**, *5*, 175–180. [CrossRef]

62. Ahmed, S.; Parsons, D. Evaluating 'ThinknLearn': A mobile science inquiry based learning application in practice. In Proceedings of the 11th International Conference on Mobile and Contextual Learning, Helsinki, Finland, 16–18 October 2012; pp. 17–24.

63. Pfeiffer, V.D.I.; Gemballa, S.; Jarodzka, H.; Scheiter, K.; Gerjets, P. Situated learning in the mobile age: Mobile devices on a field trip to the sea. *ALT-J Res. Learn. Technol.* **2009**, *17*, 187–199. [CrossRef]

MDPI

St. Alban-Anlage 66

4052 Basel

Switzerland

Tel. +41 61 683 77 34

Fax +41 61 302 89 18

www.mdpi.com

Education Sciences Editorial Office

E-mail: education@mdpi.com

www.mdpi.com/journal/education